# Becoming a
# HOMELAND
# SECURITY
# PROFESSIONAL

# Becoming a

# HOMELAND SECURITY PROFESSIONAL

LEARNINGEXPRESS®

New York

Library of Congress Cataloging-in-Publication Data:
Becoming a homeland security professional.
    p.   cm.
    ISBN 978-1-57685-750-2
    1.  United States. Dept. of Homeland Security—Vocational guidance.   2.  United States.
Dept. of Homeland Security—Officials and employees.   3.  National security—Vocational
guidance—United States.   4.  Emergency management—Vocational guidance—United
States.   5.  Law enforcement—Vocational guidance—United States.   6.  Civil defense—
Vocational guidance—United States.   I.  LearningExpress (Organization)
    HV6432.4.B43 2010
    363.34023'73—dc22

                                                                          2009036635

Printed in the United States of America

9  8  7  6  5  4  3  2  1

ISBN 978-1-57685-750-2

For more information or to place an order, contact LearningExpress at:
    2 Rector Street
    26th Floor
    New York, NY 10006

Or visit us at:
    www.learnatest.com

# Contents

# CONTENTS

# Contributors

**Mike Clumpner** is the founder and co-owner of Archangel Consulting, based in Charlotte, North Carolina. Archangel Consulting specializes in providing training and consulting in the fields of homeland security, public safety, disaster response, tactical medicine, critical care medical education, and health care. Mike is also a full-time fire captain/paramedic for the Charlotte Fire Department, where he is assigned to the Special Operations Division. He also spent five years as a tactical instructor for the United States Department of Justice, where he was responsible for creating training modules and instructing at the FBI Academy and the DEA Academy in Quantico, Virginia.

Mike has undergraduate degrees in fire science, paramedicine, and business administration, a master's degree in business administration (MBA) and is now completing a doctoral degree (PhD) in homeland security policy. He has published numerous magazine articles and books on critical care medicine and homeland security. Mike is a frequent lecturer on critical care medicine, public safety operations, and homeland security. He has lectured extensively throughout North America, Latin America, Europe, Australia, New Zealand, and the Caribbean, and has presented at over 170 congresses and symposiums.

**R. Lee Williams** is a consultant in Marine Law Enforcement/Surveillance Techniques with Archangel Consulting in Charlotte, North Carolina. At Archangel Consulting, Lee is responsible for consulting and instruction in marine law enforcement officer safety, and pirate repel at sea, as well as specializing in instructing and providing target surveillance technique.

Lee served eight years in the United States Coast Guard engaged in search and rescue, and marine law enforcement in south Florida, as well as drug interdiction throughout the Caribbean. After serving with the United States Coast Guard, Lee worked as a Marine Law Enforcement Officer with the United States Customs Service. Lee received his initial training with the Customs Service as a Criminal Investigator at the Federal Law Enforcement Training Center in Glynco, Georgia. Following his career at Customs, Lee founded two successful independent insurance agencies, and performed work as the lead investigator for a large private investigations company in Charlotte, North Carolina.

# Introduction

What do you think of when you hear the term *Department of Homeland Security*? Do you think of one department within the vast United States government? As this book helps to illustrate, the Department of Homeland Security (DHS) is much more than that.

If you've purchased this book, then something about working for the DHS appeals to you. That's a good thing, because whether you are just starting down your career path, or are looking for a mid-career change, the Department of Homeland Security holds enormous opportunity. Here's just a sample of what DHS professionals do on a daily basis:

- ▶ secure our borders and skies
- ▶ gather intelligence
- ▶ protect the infrastructure of our country
- ▶ train future federal agents, officers, and investigators
- ▶ enforce immigration laws

▶ investigate illegal importation of narcotics, artifacts, and agricultural products

▶ assist in emergency preparedness and response

▶ work in canine enforcement

▶ work in public and legal affairs, budget and finance, and human resources management

▶ investigate counterfeiting and financial crimes

▶ work to uphold civil liberties

▶ work in human resources management

▶ research and develop new technology and scientific methods utilized in the field

▶ develop and maintain emergency communications

▶ search and rescue

▶ coordinate medical activities

▶ help protect the nation and its resources against nuclear threats

▶ protect our nation's capital and government officials

▶ work in cyber security

▶ and much, much more

If any tasks in the preceding list is attractive, the DHS might have a job for you. But are you a match for the DHS? DHS professionals come from all walks of life, with different career skills, experience, and educational backgrounds. In other words, there is no singular type of person employed by the DHS—but you can get an initial idea of whether you and the DHS are a good match by answering the following questions.

## ARE YOU A UNITED STATES CITIZEN?

Almost all positions within the Department of Homeland Security will require you to be a United States citizen or a naturalized United States citizen.

## HAVE YOU EVER BEEN CONVICTED OF A FELONY?

Almost all the positions within the Department of Homeland Security will not allow you to be employed or to gain a security clearance if you have been convicted of a felony crime. If there are extreme extenuating circumstances surrounding your conviction, you may still be able to gain employment in a limited number of positions.

## HAVE YOU EVER DEFAULTED ON A GOVERNMENT-BACKED STUDENT LOAN?

The federal government prohibits hiring any individuals who have defaulted on a government-backed student loan. This is not just a Department of Homeland Security policy, but one that is recognized across the spectrum of federal employment.

## IF YOU WERE IN THE MILITARY, DID YOU RECEIVE AN HONORABLE DISCHARGE?

The DHS will not consider for employment any military personnel who received a less than honorable discharge.

## ARE YOU WILLING TO TRAVEL IN THE UNITED STATES AS WELL AS TO FOREIGN COUNTRIES?

If you like to travel in the United States as well as to foreign countries, then the Department of Homeland Security is for you. If you don't like to travel, do not worry. The Department of Homeland Security has many positions that do not require travel.

## HAVE YOU EVER BEEN CONVICTED OF BUYING, SELLING, OR TRANSPORTING ILLEGAL DRUGS?

One of the main roles of the Department of Homeland Security is to prevent the introduction of illegal drugs into the United States, and thus the DHS drug policy is very strict. Since DHS positions are considered public trust positions, the agency does not allow any employees to have convictions for buying, selling, or transporting illegal drugs.

## DO YOU CURRENTLY MAINTAIN DUAL CITIZENSHIP?

The Department of Homeland Security does not allow for any employee to maintain dual citizenship. If you are offered the job, it will be done on the contingency that you surrender your foreign citizenship. Because of the nature of the risk concerning security-sensitive information, some positions may not allow employees to have ever maintained dual citizenship after the age of 18.

## HAVE YOU EVER BEEN ISSUED A FOREIGN PASSPORT?

The Department of Homeland Security has to carefully scrutinize the potential for foreign influence in all their employees. If you possessed a foreign passport after the age of 18, you may not be eligible for some positions within the Department of Homeland Security.

## ARE YOU WILLING TO CARRY A FIREARM IN THE PERFORMANCE OF YOUR DUTIES, AND USE IT IF REQUIRED?

All sworn law enforcement positions are required to carry a firearm during the performance of their duties. If you are not willing to carry a firearm or use it during the performance of your duties, you may not want to consider a sworn law enforcement position. However, many positions within the Department of Homeland Security do not require you to carry a firearm.

## HAVE YOU EVER ILLEGALLY OR INAPPROPRIATELY REMOVED HARDWARE, SOFTWARE OR MEDIA, AND/OR INTRODUCED HARDWARE, SOFTWARE OR MEDIA INTO AN INFORMATION TECHNOLOGY SYSTEM?

Applicants will not be considered for a security clearance if they have illegally or inappropriately removed hardware, software or media, or introduced hardware, software or media into an information technology system. The Department of Homeland Security views misuse or illegal activities surrounding information technology to be a very serious threat to national security.

## HAVE YOU EVER BEEN FIRED FROM A JOB OR CONVICTED OF A CRIME INVOLVING AN INTENTIONAL BREACH OF TRUST?

An applicant who has a history of embezzlement, employee theft, check fraud, income tax evasion, expense account fraud, deceptive loan statements, or any other intentional breach of trust will be considered a security risk, and will most likely not be offered a job unless there were extreme extenuating circumstances.

## ARE YOU WILLING TO UNDERGO A COMPREHENSIVE BACKGROUND INVESTIGATION?

Many jobs within the Department of Homeland Security will require a security clearance. As part of the security clearance process, a background investigator will contact all of your past employers, your spouse (or ex-spouse) and family members, as well as many of your friends and neighbors.

## ARE YOU WILLING TO BE COMPLETELY FORTHRIGHT AND HONEST WITH ANY QUESTIONS REGARDING YOUR PAST THAT A BACKGROUND INVESTIGATOR MAY HAVE?

During the course of a background investigation, you may be asked many different questions regarding your actions in the past. You must be completely honest and candid in answering all questions. Failing to be honest and candid will result in immediate dismissal from the hiring process.

## ARE YOU WILLING TO TAKE RANDOM DRUG TESTS THROUGHOUT THE DURATION OF YOUR CAREER?

Employees with the Department of Homeland Security are required to submit to random drug tests during the duration of their employment. A positive drug test will result in dismissal from employment.

## ARE YOU WILLING TO LEARN A FOREIGN LANGUAGE?

Some positions within the Department of Homeland Security require you to speak a foreign language, such as jobs with the Border Patrol. However, if you're interested in a career with the Border Patrol, don't worry—the DHS will send you to school to learn to speak the language.

## ARE YOU WILLING TO GO THROUGH INITIAL PAID TRAINING THAT MAY BE AS LONG AS SIX MONTHS IN LENGTH?

Many positions within the Department of Homeland Security will require you to attend training before you start in your position. Some positions, including criminal investigator (special agent), require training that may even exceed six months before you actually start in your new position. This training is all paid, and if the training is not located in your city, travel and housing is usually paid for.

## ARE YOU WILLING TO FREQUENTLY ATTEND ON-THE-JOB TRAINING CLASSES, INCLUDING CLASSES HELD IN OTHER STATES?

DHS employees frequently have to attend training while at work. For many employees, this training may require travel to the Federal Law Enforcement Training Center, which is headquartered in Glynco, Georgia, with satellite campuses in Artesia, New Mexico; Charleston, South Carolina; and Cheltenham, Maryland.

## ARE YOU WILLING TO COOPERATIVELY WORK WITH OTHER AGENCIES, INCLUDING LOCAL, STATE, AND FEDERAL AGENCIES?

The Department of Homeland Security coordinates the response of over 87,000 jurisdictions. Frequently, the members of the Department of Homeland Security will work side-by-side with members from other agencies, including local and state agencies, as well as other federal agencies. It is important to be able to work cooperatively with the other agencies in order to accomplish the mission of the Department of Homeland Security.

## ARE YOU IN GOOD PHYSICAL SHAPE?

Many positions within the Department of Homeland Security require you to be in good physical shape. Because many of the jobs do not have a typical office, you may be required to perform various strenuous physical activities during the course of your duties. Some of the positions within the Department of Homeland Security will require you to pass a preemployment physical agility test prior to being hired.

Think you have what it takes to pursue a career in the DHS? Then keep reading! The first chapter of this book takes you through the evolution of what has become the largest law enforcement agency in the United States of America—the Department of Homeland Security. In Chapters 2 through 8, you will explore the myriad areas of opportunity within the DHS, to help you pinpoint the career that best fits you. Finally, in Chapters 9 through 14, we look into strategies that will help you get the job you want in the Department of Homeland Security. You've taken the first step to becoming a homeland security professional.

# CHAPTER one

## WHY HOMELAND SECURITY?

## ONE TEAM, ONE MISSION

The DHS mission statement reads:

> *We will lead the unified national effort to secure America. We will
> prevent and deter terrorist attacks and protect against and respond to
> threats and hazards to the nation. We will secure our national borders
> while welcoming lawful immigrants, visitors, and trade.*[1]

On October 8, 2001, five weeks after the 9/11 terrorist attacks on New
York City and Washington, DC, President Bush created the White House
Office of Homeland Security. A year later, on November 19, 2002, Con-
gress passed legislation mandating the Department of Homeland Security;

the DHS became operational three months after that, on January 24, 2003; and most agencies comprising the new department merged on March 1, 2003.

The creation of the DHS involved the largest reorganization of the federal government since the U.S. Department of Defense was created in 1947,[2] and its strategic plan is simple and straightforward: *"One team, one mission, securing our homeland."*[3] With over 216,000 employees, DHS is tasked with protecting the territories of the United States, patrolling our borders and ports, defending the skies, enforcing immigration laws, and responding to disasters and other significant emergencies. The career opportunities are enormous.

**QUICK FACT**

The Department of Homeland Security currently has over 216,000 employees.

## WHAT IS DHS?

The historic reorganization that marked the creation of the DHS in 2002 unified over 22 departments and agencies within the federal government and transferred agencies, personnel, assets, and obligations directly to the newly created DHS. This complete reorganization was no easy task and continues to evolve today. The following table lists the departments and agencies prior to the Homeland Security Act of 2002 and how they line up today under the DHS umbrella:

| Original Agency (Department) | Current Agency/Office |
| --- | --- |
| U.S. Customs Service (Treasury) | U.S. Customs and Border Protection<br>U.S. Immigration and Customs Enforcement |
| Immigration and Naturalization Service (Justice) | U.S. Customs and Border Protection<br>U.S. Immigration and Customs Enforcement<br>U.S. Citizenship and Immigration Services |
| Federal Protective Service | U.S. Immigration and Customs Enforcement |
| Transportation Security Administration (Transportation) | Transportation Security Administration |

| Original Agency (Department) | Current Agency/Office |
|---|---|
| Federal Law Enforcement Training Center (Treasury) | Federal Law Enforcement Training Center |
| Animal and Plant Health Inspection Service (part)(Agriculture) | U.S. Customs and Border Protection |
| Office for Domestic Preparedness (Justice) | Responsibilities distributed within FEMA |
| Federal Emergency Management Agency (FEMA) | Federal Emergency Management Agency (FEMA) |
| Strategic National Stockpile and the National Disaster Medical System (HHS) | Returned to Health and Human Services, July, 2004 |
| Nuclear Incident Response Team (Energy); Domestic Emergency Support Teams (Justice); National Domestic Preparedness Office (FBI) | Responsibilities distributed within FEMA |
| Chemical, Biological, Radiological, and Nuclear (CBRN) Countermeasures Programs (Energy); Environmental Measurements Laboratory (Energy); National BW Defense Analysis Center (Defense); Plum Island Animal Disease Center (Agriculture) | Science & Technology Directorate |
| Federal Computer Incident Response Center (GSA) | US-CERT, Office of Cybersecurity and Communications in the National Programs and Preparedness Directorate |
| National Communications System (Defense) | Office of Cybersecurity and Communications in the National Programs and Preparedness Directorate |
| National Infrastructure Protection Center (FBI) | Dispersed throughout the department, including Office of Operations Coordination and Office of Infrastructure Protection |
| Energy Security and Assurance Program (Energy) | Integrated into the Office of Infrastructure Protection |
| U.S. Coast Guard | U.S. Coast Guard |
| U.S. Secret Service | U.S. Secret Service |

The following three directorates, created by the Homeland Security Act of 2002, were abolished by a reorganization in July 2005 and their responsibilities were transferred to other departmental components:

Border and Transportation Security

Emergency Preparedness and Response

Information Analysis and Infrastructure Protection

## DEPARTMENTS WITHIN THE DEPARTMENT

The Department of Homeland Security has coordinated the resources at the federal, state, and local level, integrating over 87,000 different jurisdictions. To know where you may fit in the vast undertakings of DHS, you need to know what each department of DHS does and compare them to your career interests. Here are the major components that currently make up DHS.[4]

The **Directorate for National Protection and Programs** works to advance the Department's risk-reduction mission. Reducing risk requires an integrated approach that encompasses both physical and virtual threats and their associated human elements. This department provides cyber and communication security, resiliency, and reliability, protection of the nation's infrastructure, promotion of intergovernmental cooperation, national risk management and analysis, and biometrics-based technologies.

The **Directorate for Science and Technology** is the primary research and development arm of the DHS. It maintains partnerships with the private sector, national laboratories and universities, and other governmental agencies both foreign and domestic. The Directorate for Science and Technology is discussed in further detail in Chapter 2.

The **Directorate for Management** is responsible for DHS budgets and appropriations, expenditure of funds, accounting and finance, procurement, and human resources. The Directorate for Management also provides information technology systems, facilities and equipment, and the identification and tracking of performance measurements.

The **Office of Policy** is the primary policy formulation and coordination component of DHS. It provides a centralized, coordinated focus to the development of department-wide, long-range planning to protect the United States through coordinated development; strategic planning; coordination with federal, state, and local law enforcement; international affairs; immigration statistics; and private sector communication. It also provides advice to support decisions involving global actions.

The **Office of Health Affairs** coordinates all medical activities of DHS to ensure appropriate preparation for and response to incidents having medical significance. The Office of Health Affairs provides bio-monitoring, emergency management and response, safety and personnel programs, and global health security.

The **Office of Intelligence and Analysis** is responsible for using information and intelligence from multiple sources to identify and assess current and future threats related to border security, threats of radicalization and extremism, threats from particular groups entering the United States, and threats to the critical infrastructure and key resources. The office collects, analyzes, and disseminates information and intelligence, and provides training to federal, state, and local governmental personnel. It also partners with governmental agencies to address their hazard information needs, and assists with the development and implementation of effective information-sharing policies.

The **Office of Operations Coordination** is responsible for monitoring the security of the United States through intelligence and law enforcement. The intelligence side focuses on pieces of highly classified intelligence and how this intelligence contributes to the current threat picture. The law enforcement side is dedicated to tracking the different enforcement activities across nations that may have a connection, tie, or link to terrorists. This information gathering and tracking is conducted on a daily basis and activities are coordinated within the department as well as with governors, homeland security advisors, law enforcement partners, and critical infrastructure operators in all 50 states, and more than 50 major urban areas nationwide.

The **Federal Law Enforcement Training Center (FLETC)** provides career-long training to law enforcement professionals to help them fulfill their responsibilities safely and proficiently. The FLETC serves as an interagency training center for more than 80 federal agencies and also provides services to state, local, and international law enforcement agencies. The FLETC is headquartered in Glynco, Georgia, and also has training sites in Artesia, New Mexico, and Charleston, South Carolina. The FLETC also provides oversight and management for the International Law Enforcement Academy in foreign lands.

The **Domestic Nuclear Detection Office** works to enhance the nuclear detection efforts of federal, state, territorial, tribal, and local governments as well as the private sector, and to ensure a coordinated response to threats. This includes conducting research and development, determining vulnerabilities, providing information, and sharing forensics capabilities. This Office also detects and reports unauthorized attempts to import, possess, store, develop, and transport nuclear or radiological material.

The **Transportation Security Administration (TSA)** protects the nation's transportation systems to ensure freedom of movement for people and commerce. It provides security screening of passengers and luggage, federal air marshals, pilot and flight crew training, trucking security programs, port security training, explosives detection canine teams, freight rail programs, and bus security programs.

**United States Customs and Border Protection (CBP)** is responsible for protecting and controlling our nation's borders and is one of the largest, most complex components of DHS. This office enforces the laws against human and drug smuggling, illegal migration, and agricultural pests. CBP also facilitates trade through import and export.

**United States Citizenship and Immigration Services** is responsible for the administration of immigration and naturalization adjudication functions and for establishing immigration services policies and priorities. This office oversees citizenship, residency, employment authorization, adoptions, asylum, refugee status, and student authorization.

**United States Immigration and Customs Enforcement (ICE)** is the largest investigative arm of the DHS. ICE is responsible for identifying and shutting down vulnerabilities in the nation's border, economic, transportation, and infrastructure security. ICE investigates the following: drug trafficking, immigration and customs fraud, child pornography, financial crimes, intellectual property rights violations, sexual predators, visa security, document and identity fraud, and illegal arms trafficking.

The **United States Coast Guard (USCG)** is a military, multimission maritime service. It protects the public, the environment, and United States economic interests in the nation's ports and waterways, along the coast, on international waters, or in any maritime region as required in support of national security. The USCG also provides maritime safety and security, and facilitates commerce of goods and services as well as protection of natural services. The Coast Guard is also tasked with national defense as one of the five United States armed services.

The **Federal Emergency Management Agency (FEMA)** prepares the nation for hazards and manages federal response and recovery efforts following any national incident. This office also administers the National Flood Insurance Program. The Federal Emergency Management Agency provides service to disaster victims, operational emergency planning, incident management, disaster logistics, hazard mitigation, emergency communications, and integrated preparedness.

The **United States Secret Service (USSS)** protects the president and other high-level officials. The Secret Service investigates counterfeiting and other financial crimes, including financial institution fraud, identity theft, and computer fraud; it also investigates computer-based attacks on United States financial, banking, and telecommunications infrastructure.

The **Office of the Secretary** oversees activities with other federal, state, local, and private entities as part of a collaborative effort to strengthen our borders, provide for intelligence analysis and infrastructure protection, improve the use of science and technology to counter weapons of mass destruction, and create a comprehensive response and recovery system. The Office of the Secretary includes multiple offices that contribute to the overall homeland security mission, all of which are discussed in more detail in the following chapter.

## ADVISORY PANELS AND COMMITTEES

The **Homeland Security Advisory Council** provides advice and recommendations to the secretary of DHS on matters related to homeland security. The council is comprised of leaders from state and local government, first responder communities, the private sector, and academia.

The **National Infrastructure Advisory Council** provides advice to the president of the United States through the secretary of homeland security on the security of information systems for the public and private institutions that constitute the critical infrastructure of the United States economy.

The **Homeland Security Science and Technology Advisory Committee** serves as a source of independent scientific and technical planning advice for the undersecretary for science and technology.

The **Critical Infrastructure Partnership Advisory Council** was established to facilitate effective coordination between federal infrastructure protection programs with the infrastructure protection activities of the private sector and of state, local, territorial, and tribal governments.

The **Interagency Coordinating Council on Emergency Preparedness and Individuals with Disabilities** was established to ensure that the federal government appropriately supports safety and security for individuals with disabilities in disaster situations.

The **Task Force on New Americans** is an interagency effort to help immigrants learn English, embrace the common core of American civic culture, and fully integrate into society.

As you can see, the DHS utilizes a whole array of support staff to carry out their mission and encompasses a wide spectrum of career possibilities. This diversity, combined with today's economy, makes the DHS an attractive and secure career option for qualified individuals.

## DIVERSITY

Minority representation in the federal government far exceeds the participation found in the private sector. In particular, the Hispanic and Latino minority population is a valuable asset to DHS, especially along our southern borders. According to the Department of Labor, at 18.9% Hispanics and Latinos are represented more in DHS than in other government agency or department.[5]

**QUICK FACT**

Hispanics and Latinos make up 18.9% of the DHS workforce, the largest concentration in any United States agency.

The federal government leads the private sector in hiring women, as well, and is a particularly attractive option for family-minded career women. The Bureau of Labor Statistics states that 53.2% of the federal government utilizes a flex schedule, compared to the private sector where flex scheduling is found less than 37% of the time.[6] If you have a family, then a federal career with flex scheduling may be just the thing you have been looking for.

If you are a veteran of the armed forces, the federal government wants your discipline, dedication to public service, skills, and training. The DHS seeks former military personnel and provides veterans with up to ten preference points on application scores.

If you think having a disability will not allow you to work with DHS, think again. The federal government has paved the way in hiring people with disabilities. Chapter 2 discusses this topic in more detail.

The needs of the federal government and, in particular, those found within DHS create endless possibilities. Eighty-seven percent of the jobs in the federal government are located outside the Washington, DC area.[7] Whether your interests lie in the maritime environment, the Southwest border or Canadian border, our nation's capital, or any place in between, the DHS likely has a position located in an area of the United States that will appeal to you. If you are interested in foreign travel, DHS also has positions located outside the United States.

The federal government serves as a model to the private sector in achieving workplace diversity and the DHS can provide individuals with a myriad of employment opportunities that you may have thought were out of reach.

**QUICK FACT**

Eighty-seven percent of the jobs in the federal government are located outside of Washington, DC.

## TODAY'S ECONOMY

Due to the nation's recent spike in unemployment, fewer private businesses are expanding and many are downsizing. Conversely, the federal stimulus package has created an increased number of job opportunities within DHS, and federal pay takes the economic climate into account, with annual cost-of-living increases and locality pay adjustments called COLA. These adjustments amounted to a 3.9 cost-of-living increase in 2009; based on figures released by the Department of Labor, it is slated to increase over 2.9 percent further in 2010.

For anyone looking for a career with relative stability, the federal government has become a much more attractive option than the private sector for job security and satisfaction.

## PROJECTIONS FOR THE FUTURE

Although no one can accurately predict what the future will hold for job prospects within DHS, the trend is for the government to increase personnel as the need for services increases. Currently, the federal government employs 2.1% of the nation's total workforce, and this number is projected to grow by 2.5% through 2014.[8]

According to *Where the Jobs Are, Mission Critical Opportunities for America*, published by the Partnership for Public Service, the federal government's greatest hiring need is in security enforcement and compliance assistance careers. With more than 8,000 miles of international land and water boundaries to protect, it is no surprise that the DHS is expected to extensively hire in the areas of border control and airport security. The single largest increases are in the occupational categories of criminal and noncritical investigators, inspectors, police officers, security and prison guards, transportation safety officers, customs and border patrol officers, immigration agents, and intelligence analysts. We look further into these careers in Chapter 2.

In addition to the creation of new jobs within DHS, recent federal reports estimate that 42% of today's federal employees will be reaching retirement age by the year 2010, and those vacancies will need to be filled.[9]

### QUICK FACT

Forty-two percent of today's federal employee workforce will be eligible to retire in the year 2016.

## IF YOU ARE JUST STARTING YOUR CAREER

The DHS offers recent college grads job security, excellent benefits, and, most importantly, a future as an integral part of the protection and future of our nation. The federal government offers attractive hiring incentives to recent grads, such as recruitment bonuses and student loan repayments. The student loan repayment program can help recent grads repay student loans, paying up to $10,000 per year to a total of $60,000. This incentive can be important when you are considering loan repayment options; however, there are some stipulations, such as minimum length of service requirements. Government incentive programs are discussed in further detail in later chapters.

Just starting or not yet finished with college? The federal government offers summer jobs, internships, and volunteer programs to college students. These programs can help you discover your interests and build contacts within the federal government, and provide valuable work experience related to your academic program. These available programs can help you find the right federal career.

## IF YOU ARE LOOKING FOR A MIDCAREER CHANGE

As we just learned, more than 40% of current full-time federal employees will retire by 2016, which will leave a critical void in experienced leaders. The federal government will look to the private sector to fill that need, which creates an unprecedented opportunity for those looking for a mid-career change. If you are currently employed in the private sector you may be able to bring your experience and leadership, along with fresh ideas, into DHS.

For those already employed by the federal government who are looking for a less stressful or more challenging position in leadership, the DHS, with its diverse responsibilities, can offer a large pool of new career-changing opportunities. This book contains the tools necessary to help you discover (or rediscover) your interests and guide you through the application process. If you have been employed in the federal government for any length of time, you may need to brush up on how to reapply, as the application process may have changed. The federal application process is covered in depth in Chapter 11.

**QUICK FACT**

DHS is in need of experienced professionals from the private sector, even retired or semiretired individuals.

Now that we have discussed a little of what the Department of Homeland Security has to offer, it is time to explore in depth the actual job opportunities available so you can discover your perfect homeland security career match.

# CHAPTER two

## MISSION SUPPORT CAREERS

**IN THIS** chapter we take a deeper look into careers that make up the behind-the-scenes jobs at DHS—mission support. The careers found in mission support make up the critical infrastructure of the organization, and without these personnel, those on the front lines would not be able to perform their tasks. Careers in mission support can be found in management, human resources, Internet technology, engineering, accounting, sciences, research, communication, and much more.

Let us look at each department that has careers in mission support. While reviewing what each department does, think about how your interests and abilities may fit into a future career.

## OFFICE OF THE SECRETARY

The Office of the Secretary is headed by the secretary of DHS and identifies the goals and objectives of DHS. The Office of the Secretary oversees activities pertaining to DHS and coordinates, integrates, and centralizes those activities through sound and cohesive management. It brings together federal, state, and local governments with a unified mission to secure the United States and preserve its freedoms without a duplication of efforts. The focus of this office is to sharpen operational effectiveness in delivering services in support of DHS.

**QUICK FACT**

Scientific professionals within DHS research and develop new technology utilized by federal, state, and local governments, as well as the private sector.

## DIRECTORATE FOR SCIENCE AND TECHNOLOGY

As the primary research and development arm of DHS, this office encourages and sustains an integrated basic research enterprise to produce the fundamental scientific understanding and technology needed to meet current and future requirements of DHS. The Directorate of Science and Technology focuses on enabling its personnel to carry out the vital missions of DHS. These personnel include the field agents, inspectors, members of the Coast Guard, airport screeners and federal air marshals, as well as state, local, and federal emergency responders, and many others.

The Directorate for Science and Technology maintains a portfolio of six basic focus research areas:

1. Explosives Division
2. Chemical and Biological Division
3. Command and Control Interoperability Division
4. Infrastructure and Geophysical Division
5. Human Factors/Behavioral Sciences Division
6. Borders and Maritime Division

The mission of the **Explosives Division** is to provide, through research and development, the detection and countermeasure techniques and technology necessary to protect the nation against the malicious use of explosives. It accomplishes this mission through improved informatics and design for biological and chemical analysis, highly accurate sampling, assays, instruments, data analysis, storage interoperability, preservation, decision tools, and response and recovery research, as well as through education programs to support graduate student research in science, technology, engineering, and mathematics disciplines.

The focus of the **Chemical and Biological Division** is to increase the nation's preparedness against chemical and biological threats through improved threat awareness, advanced surveillance, detection and protective countermeasures, response and restoration programs, and forensics. The Chemical and Biological Division works closely with DHS's Office of Health Affairs and chief medical officer as well as the Office of Infrastructure, increasing awareness of public and governmental security threats and their response to them.

The **Command and Control Interoperability Division** works with other federal, state, and local governments as well as private business to create and deploy information resources to strengthen communications interoperability, improve Internet security, and develop automated capabilities to help identify potential national threats. This division also leads cybersecurity research as well as the development, testing, and evaluation necessary to secure the United States' future critical cyber infrastructure. We look a lot more closely at cybersecurity careers in the Chapter 6.

## QUICK FACT

The Department of Homeland Security protects the United States from the hazards of natural and manmade threats including terrorism, hurricanes, flooding, and tornados.

The mission of the **Infrastructure and Geophysical Division** is to improve and increase the nation's preparedness for and response to natural and man-made threats through situational awareness, emergency response capabilities, and critical infrastructure protection. This division's primary areas of concern are:

▶ critical infrastructure protection (banking, energy, water, healthcare, nuclear materials, transportation systems, and national monuments and icons)

▶ preparedness and response (saving lives, minimizing damage, and restoring critical services)

▶ geophysical concerns (natural catastrophes, hurricanes, floods, and earthquakes)

In addition, this division develops technical solutions and modeling and simulation tools to improve the hazard response of federal, state, and local governmental agencies, and aids in private business preparation.

The **Human Factors/Behavioral Sciences Division** develops and applies social, behavioral, and physical sciences to better understand terrorist motivation, intent, and behavior. This division's major thrust areas are in:

▶ personal identification systems
▶ human technology integration
▶ social and behavioral threat analysis

The Human Factors/Behavioral Sciences Division works to improve the identification and analysis of threats, but also to enhance societal resilience and integrate human capabilities into the development of technologies. They accomplish this through improved screening processes to identify deceptive and suspicious behavior; the development and use of biometrics; and through credentialing tools, building safety, and utilizing public input.

**QUICK FACT**

The Department of Homeland Security is the nation's first line of defense for the United States borders, including its maritime and aviation interests.

The mission of the **Borders and Maritime Division** is to protect the security of the United States borders and waterways without impeding the flow of commerce and travelers. This is accomplished by developing technologies and methods to detect dangerous individuals and materials and prevent them from entering the United States. This includes advanced screening and targeting, risk assessment, analysis of the supply chain, automated imagery detection capabilities, and both intrusive and nonintrusive search technologies. This division also increases officer safety through facial recognition technologies, surveillance capabilities, gunfire location detection, less lethal countermeasures, and ballistics protection.

## Other Offices

The Directorate for Science and Technology also include:

▶ The **Office of Business Operations, Services, and Human Capital**, which serves to provide human capital resources, financial planning, management, monitoring, and logistical support for science and technology operations and research.

▶ The **Office of Corporate Communications**, which serves to provide the necessary infrastructure and flow of communications throughout the Directorate of Science and Technology.

▶ The **Office of Homeland Security Institute**, which serves to address important homeland security issues, particularly those requiring scientific, technical, and analytical expertise utilizing think tank concepts.

▶ The **Office of Interagency and First Responders Programs**, which serves to coordinate joint science and technology programs of national scope and impact.

▶ The **Office of International Cooperative Programs**, which serves to match DHS research, development, testing, and evaluation with the international community through cooperative research activities.

▶ The **Office of Operations Analysis Division**, which serves to manage federally funded research and development centers, evaluating and validating competing concepts of operations, new system concepts, and ongoing projects.

▶ The **Office of Policy and Budget Division**, which serves to provide fiscal management of appropriations under science and technology, and the financial administration of all its programs.

▶ The **Office of Special Programs**, which serves to provide programmatic leadership and direction in programs that are deemed especially sensitive, classified, or deserving of extraordinary security protection in the areas of emerging threats, risk sciences, intelligence, surveillance and reconnaissance, and special access.

▶ The **Office of Test and Evaluation Standards**, which serves to establish policies and programs to support the development, coordination, and operational management of test and evaluation standards.

## OFFICE OF INTELLIGENCE AND ANALYSIS

The Office of Intelligence and Analysis (I&A) provides intelligence and information to the secretary of DHS and federal officials, as well as to local and private sector partners. Under DHS, I&A comprises the intelligence elements of the following DHS components:

▶ Citizenship and Immigration Services
▶ United States Coast Guard
▶ Customs and Border Protection
▶ Immigration and Customs Enforcement
▶ Transportation Security Administration

The key areas of intelligence and analysis focus on threats relating to border security; radicalization and extremism; suspect groups entering the United States; critical infrastructure and key resources; and weapons of mass destruction as well as health threats. The I&A provides intelligence training to DHS and many others. The I&A partners with state and local governments as well as the private sector to gather information by creating state and local fusion centers that provide officials with situational awareness. Its principles are to change the intelligence culture from "need to know" to "responsibility to provide," which enhances the core capabilities of requirements, analysis, and dissemination. The I&A is committed to attracting a world-class workforce in the future to ensure continued success in the business of providing homeland security.

**QUICK FACT**

The Department of Homeland Security coordinates efforts with other federal agencies as well as state, local, and tribal governments.

## OFFICE OF OPERATIONS COORDINATION

The Office of Operations Coordination works to deter, detect, and prevent terrorist acts by coordinating federal, state, local, and private sector partners. This office coordinates activities related to incident management, and employs all the departmental resources to translate intelligence and policy into action. The Office of Operations Coordination oversees the National Operations Center, which collects and disseminates information to more than 35 federal, state, territorial, tribal, local, and private sector agencies.

## OFFICE FOR CIVIL RIGHTS AND CIVIL LIBERTIES

The Office for Civil Rights and Civil Liberties provides advice to the secretary and senior officers of DHS on a full range of civil rights and civil liberties issues. This office's guidelines are designed to facilitate the information sharing of terrorist, weapons of mass destruction, and homeland security information while ensuring that information privacy and other legal rights of Americans are protected. Specific areas of focus within the office include improving emergency preparedness for individuals with disabilities and updating and strengthening racial profiling training of law enforcement personnel. The office investigates and resolves complaints concerning abuses of civil rights, civil liberties, and profiling on the basis of race, ethnicity, or religion by employees and officials of DHS. The office also develops and directs DHS's equal employment opportunity programs.

## OFFICE OF INSPECTOR GENERAL

The Office of Inspector General (OIG) ensures the integrity and efficiency of DHS. It serves as an independent and objective body, conducting and supervising inspections, audits, and investigations intended to promote effectiveness, efficiency, and economy, as well as to prevent fraud, abuse, mismanagement, and waste in programs, personnel, and operations. The OIG reports assist the secretary of DHS in the development of efficient cost savings, compliance with laws and regulations, and accountability throughout DHS. The OIG also assists in future planning for the needs of DHS by outlining its capabilities and shortfalls.

## DOMESTIC NUCLEAR DETECTION OFFICE

The Domestic Nuclear Detection Office (DNDO) is tasked with the responsibility of developing a global nuclear detection architecture, conducting research and development, and acquiring and supporting the deployment of domestic nuclear detection systems.

The DNDO accomplishes this by further delegating responsibilities within the department to eight different offices:

1. **The Office of Architecture Directorate** determines gaps and vulnerabilities in the existing global nuclear detection architecture. This office then formulates recommendations and plans for developing an enhanced architecture.

2. **The Office of Mission Management Directorate** manages DNDO programs in key mission areas including: ports of entry, general aviation, maritime, and domestic interior.

3. **The Office of Product Acquisition and Development Directorate** carries out the engineering development, production, developmental logistics, procurement, and development of current and next-generation nuclear detection systems.

4. **The Office of Transformational and Applied Research Directorate** conducts, supports, coordinates, and encourages aggressive, long-term research and developmental programs to address significant architecture and technical challenges unresolved by research and development efforts on the near horizon. This office sponsors research with the national laboratories and private industry to explore innovative detection materials and concepts.

5. **The Office of Operations Support Directorate** develops information sharing and analytical tools necessary to create a fully integrated operating environment. This is accomplished through a joint operations center staffed with employees from the Department of Defense, Department of Energy, Federal Bureau of Investigation, and Nuclear Regulatory Commission. This office also conducts training with federal, state, and local law enforcement and emergency responders and holds exercises to evaluate equipment and alarm adjudication processes.

6. **The Office of Systems Engineering and Evaluation Directorate** ensures that DNDO proposes sound technical solutions and thoroughly understands systems performance and vulnerabilities prior to deploying those technologies. This office sets technical capability standards and implements a test and evaluation program to provide performance, suitability, and survivability information, and related testing, for preventive radiological and nuclear detection equipment in the United States.

7. **The Office of Red Teaming and Net Assessments** independently assesses the operational performance of planned and deployed capabilities, including technologies, procedures, and protocols. Red teaming is the practice of viewing a problem from a competitor's perspective.

8. **The Office of National Technical Nuclear Forensics Center** provides national-level stewardship, centralized planning, and integration to increase national technical nuclear forensics capabilities.

## NATIONAL PROTECTION AND PROGRAMS DIRECTORATE

The National Protection and Programs Directorate (NPPD) oversees the safeguards of critical information systems and high-risk critical infrastructure such as telecommunications assets, and leads DHS cybersecurity programs for the federal government and the private sector. (Careers in cybersecurity are discussed in depth in Chapter 6.) This office also facilitates DHS in identity management and biometrics services, and it coordinates risk management methodologies across DHS. NPPD also works with state, local, and private-sector partners to identify threats, determine vulnerabilities, and target resources toward the greatest risks.

The National Protection and Programs Directorate is divided into the following five divisions:

1. **The Office of Cybersecurity and Communications (CS&C)** is responsible for enhancing the security, resiliency, and reliability of the United States' cyber and communications infrastructure. The CS&C

actively engages the public and private sector, as well as international partners, to prepare, prevent, and respond to catastrophic incidents that could degrade or overwhelm these strategic assets.

2. **The Office of Infrastructure Protection (IP)** leads a coordinated national program to reduce risks to the United States' critical infrastructure and key resources posed by acts of terrorism, and to strengthen United States preparedness, timely response, and rapid recovery in the event of an attack, natural disaster, or other emergency. The IP's mission is to identify and analyze threats and vulnerabilities; coordinate federal, state, local, territorial, and private entities that share information and resources; and mitigate risks and effects.

3. **The Office of Intergovernmental Programs (IGP)** facilitates timely and meaningful consultation by DHS and its agencies with state, local, tribal, and territorial partners. The IGP carries this out by facilitating communication, acting as advocate, and coordinating· and advancing a liaison between DHS expert resources and the expert resources of United States autonomous governments.

4. **The Office of Risk Management and Analysis (RMA)** is responsible for synchronizing, integrating, and coordinating risk management and risk analysis approaches within DHS. The RMA serves as DHS's executive agent for national level risk management analysis, standards, and metrics, developing a coordinated, collaborative effort that will allow DHS to leverage and integrate risk expertise across its components and external shareholders.

5. **The Office of US-VISIT** is charged with protecting the United States from dangerous persons. To accomplish their mission, the front line personnel in DHS must be able to accurately identify individuals they encounter and assess whether they pose a risk. This office provides biometrics identification and analysis services (such as digital fingerprinting and photographs) that enable enhanced security to citizens of the United States and its visitors, facilitates legitimate travel and trade, ensures the integrity of the DHS immigration system, and protects the privacy of visitors to the United States.

## OFFICE OF COUNTERNARCOTICS ENFORCEMENT

The Office of Counternarcotics Enforcement (CNE) coordinates policy and operations to stop the entry of illegal drugs into the United States. The responsibilities of the director of the Office of Counternarcotics Enforcement include:

▶ coordinating policy and operations within DHS, between DHS and other federal departments and agencies, and between DHS and state and local agencies with respect to stopping the entry of illegal drugs into the United States

▶ ensuring the adequacy of resources within DHS for stopping the entry of illegal drugs into the United States

▶ recommending the appropriate financial and personnel resources necessary to help DHS better fulfill its responsibility to stop the entry of illegal drugs into the United States

▶ constructing, tracking, and severing connections between drug trafficking and terrorism within the Joint Terrorism Task Force (JTTF)

▶ representing DHS on all task forces, comities, or other entities whose purpose is to coordinate the counternarcotics enforcement activities of DHS and other federal, state, or local agencies

## THE MANAGEMENT DIRECTORATE

The Management Directorate is responsible for the administration of the budget, appropriations, fund expenditures, accounting and finance, procurement, acquisitions, human resources, and enterprise-wide learning and development. With 216,000 employees,[1] they are tasked with personnel, facilities, property, equipment, and other material resources. The Management Directorate is also responsible for the security of DHS personnel, information technology and communications systems, grants, and other assistance programs. The office identifies and tracks performance measures relating to DHS. The Management Directorate is divided into the following: Office of Administrative Services, Office of Financial Management,

Office of Human Capital, Office of Information, Office of Procurement, and Office of Security.

## OFFICE OF HEALTH AFFAIRS

The Office of Health Affairs (OHA) supports and advises DHS on medical issues related to natural disasters, acts of terrorism, and other man-made disasters. It oversees DHS biodefense activities; it also leads a coordinated national architecture for biological and chemical weapons of mass destruction planning and catastrophic incident management. The Office of Health Affairs also ensures DHS employees have an effective occupational health and safety program. The OHA is comprised of the following four offices:

1. **The Office of Mass Destruction and Biodefense** leads DHS's biological and chemical defense activities in coordination with other departments and agencies across the federal government. This office integrates the biomonitoring activities of executive branch departments that include: biosurveillance, aerosol detection, environmental animal surveillance, clinical syndrome detection, mail room observation, and suspicious substance management. The Office of Mass Destruction and Biodefense accomplishes this mission as follows:

   ▶ The **National Biosurveillance Integration Center** integrates the biomonitoring activities to provide a biological common operating picture to facilitate early detection of adverse events and trends.

   ▶ **Food, Agriculture, and Veterinary Defense** ensures awareness, readiness, and response to all disasters related to food, animals, agriculture, and their impact on public health.

   ▶ **Threats and Countermeasures** utilizes material threat assessments and population threat assessments to identify medical countermeasures.

   ▶ **Early Detection** provides bioaerosol environmental monitoring systems in the largest population centers of the United States for early detection of biological agents.

▶ **Chemical Defense** provides leadership and direction to assist the United States in preparedness against a chemical attack and ensure the execution of an effective response.

2. The **Office of Medical Readiness** develops policies and programs to enhance all hazards planning, exercises, and training. This office oversees the weapons of mass destruction incident support and management, and promotes the integration of state and local medical response capabilities. The Office of Medical Readiness leads DHS in contingency planning and consequence management health and medical aspects of: biological, chemical, radiological, and nuclear hazards.

The Office of Medical Readiness is comprised of the following divisions:

▶ The **Planning and Policy Division** provides planning for scenarios, identifies health and medical impacts, and develops courses of action to mitigate those impacts. This Division builds integration, synchronization, and coordination of strategic planning activities.

▶ The **Medical First Responder Coordination Division** leads DHS in improving medical first responders' readiness for catastrophic incidents and serves as the principle representative to the medical first responders' community. This division identifies first responders' best practices and provides guidance and support for the implementation of those practices.

▶ The **Incident Coordination Division** provides incident management and guidance through coordination of all DHS goals and mandates for planning and responding to health-related issues during disasters, mass casualty incidents, and national special security events.

▶ The **Grants Coordination Division** leads interagency alignment of health preparedness grants, by identifying and addressing gaps in resources identified through DHS's planning process. The Division works to enhance training and exercise resources to meet health and medical needs of federal, state, and local agencies.

▶ The **Emergency Management and Medical Response Integration Division** facilitates integration of emergency management and medical response capabilities at the regional, state, and local levels as well as the private sector to leverage resources. This division works to enhance emergency preparedness systems for effectively responding to a public health crisis caused by, for example, weapons of mass destruction, pandemic influenza, and biodefense elements.

**QUICK FACT**

The Department of Homeland Security is the lead agency for the federal government in the training and coordination of medical first responders for all levels of government.

3.  The **Office of Component Services** leads the initiatives that support DHS's employee health and workplace protection. It provides medical oversight for health care delivery and operational medicine to save lives when preparing for and responding to natural or man-made incidents. This is accomplished by supporting DHS incident response capabilities, protecting the workforce, and providing effective occupational medicine, health, and safety programs. The Office of Component Services carries this out by creating and establishing consistent standards for emergency medical care delivered, as well as providing physician medical oversight, general and specific treatment protocols, and education and training standards. The Office of Component Services works to ensure that DHS employees are able to protect themselves from exposure to hazardous material and persons as they interact with travelers, screen cargo, and patrol the nation's waterways and borders.

4.  The **Office of International Affairs and Global Health Security (IAGHS)** serves as the subject matter expert on all aspects of global health security, natural and man-made global health threats, international medical readiness, and all hazardous emergency public health planning. This office coordinates DHS lessons learned and best practices in the areas of biodefense and health preparedness by collecting and sharing international global health security-related activities with key multinational, multilateral, bilateral, academic, and private sector

partners. The IAGHS provides international advice and coordination to three Office of Health Affairs offices as well as other federal agencies.

## PRIVACY OFFICE

The Privacy Office is the first statutory required office at any federal agency. Its mission is to minimize the impact on the individual's privacy, in particular the individual's personal information and dignity, while achieving the missions of DHS. The office centralizes Freedom of Information Act and Privacy Act operations, providing oversight and support.

The Privacy Office operates within the framework of the following privacy laws:

► **The Privacy Act of 1974** embodies a code of fair information principles that govern the collection, maintenance, use, and dissemination of personally identifiable information by federal agencies.

► **The E-Governmental Act of 2002** mandates privacy impact assessments for all federal agencies when there are new collections or new technologies applied to personally identifiable information.

► **The Freedom of Information Act of 2002** implements the principles that people have a fundamental right to know what their government is doing.

► **The Homeland Security Act of 2002** created the Chief Privacy Officer at DHS, with responsibilities to ensure that privacy and transparency in government are implemented throughout DHS.

► **The 9/11 Commission Act of 2007** amends the Homeland Security Act to give new authorities to the chief privacy officer.

## OFFICE OF LEGISLATIVE AFFAIRS

The Office of Legislative Affairs serves as primary liaison to members of Congress and their staffs, the White House and executive branch, and to other federal agencies and governmental entities that have roles in ensuring national security. The office responds to inquires from Congress and the White House, and notifies Congress about DHS initiatives, policies, and programs. The Office of Legislative Affairs also keeps other governmental bodies informed concerning homeland security measures that affect their operations and DHS actions in jointly undertaken security endeavors.

## OFFICE OF THE GENERAL COUNSEL

The Office of the General Counsel is the chief legal advisor to the Secretary of DHS and chief legal officer for the Department of Homeland Security. The general counsel and staff ensure that DHS activities comply with all legal requirements, as well as integrate the attorneys and staff throughout DHS into a cohesive full-service legal team.

Attorneys from the Office of General Counsel and its major components play major roles in crafting, developing, and defending policies relating to many of the most important issues facing the United States today including counterterrorism, immigration, border security, emergency response, and recovery, as well as countless other legal matters. The Office of General Counsel is discussed in detail in Chapter 7.

## OFFICE OF PUBLIC AFFAIRS

The Office of Public Affairs is responsible for ensuring that the public and press are informed about the Department of Homeland Security's activities and about the priorities and policies of its components. The office advises the secretary of DHS and the departments on all aspects of media relations and communication issues. Primary responsibilities of the office include: preparing communications strategies, media relations, publications review, and photographic services. The Office of Public Affairs prepares and issues DHS news releases and reviews and approves those issued by its component departments. It serves reporters assigned to the DHS by responding to inquiries, issuing news releases and statements, arranging interviews, and conducting news conferences. The office ensures that information provided to the news media by DHS is current, complete, and accurate. It also ensures that all applicable laws, regulations, and policies involving release of information to the public are followed so that the maximum disclosure is made without jeopardizing investigations and prosecutions, violating the rights of others, or compromising homeland security.

## CITIZEN AND IMMIGRATION SERVICES OMBUDSMEN

The Citizen and Immigrations Services Ombudsmen, mandated by the Homeland Security Act of 2002, provide recommendations for resolving issues between the individual and the United States Citizenship and Immigration Services department. This is an independent office that acts as an intermediary between DHS and the rights of the individual in dealings with the department. The division's job is to investigate complaints of improper governmental activities against an individual. Ombudsmen also serve to identify areas in which individuals and employers have problems dealing with the department, and propose changes. The Citizen and Immigrations Services Ombudsmen also attempt to resolve any problems through recommendations or mediation.

## CAREERS IN MISSION SUPPORT

Now that you have seen just what the components are that make up mission support careers in DHS, let us look at some typical careers in mission support. This listing is in no way meant to be all-inclusive—it would be prohibitive to list each and every career available in the missions support career field. This sampling of available careers should stimulate your interests so you will research what DHS has available, then assess your skills to see where they might fit.

Careers in mission support are spread throughout the Department of Homeland Security's 22 agencies and departments. Higher educational career specialties may be limited to those agencies that specialize in that particular field.

## CAREER SNAPSHOTS

**Who:** Information Technology Specialist

**What:** Is responsible for the coordination and implementation of Information Technology security programs. Serves as project leader coordinating, planning, analyzing, and developing solutions to problems related to automated information system security. Administers system requirements to ensure compliance as well as the technical aspects of integration and configuration of systems in the enterprise architecture and compliance enforcement activities associated with information technology security policies and procedures.

**Where:** Information Technology Specialist careers are found throughout the DHS's agencies.

---

**Who:** Physical Scientist

**What:** Coordinates, analyzes, researches, and provides technical support for continued development, acquisition, logistics, and fielding of high-tech large and/or complex inspections, surveillance, and investigative systems and equipment during the research, development, testing, and evaluation acquisition or support phase.

**Where:** Physical Scientist careers are found primarily within the Directorate of Science and Technology and the U.S. Coast Guard.

---

**Who:** Human Resources Specialist (Labor Relations)

**What:** Serves to apply expert knowledge and mastery of labor relations and advanced human resource principles, concepts, regulations, practices, analytical methods, and techniques to develop and implement a labor relations program. Also facilitates communications with union representatives and provides advice on matters relating to labor relations issues, acting as the expert on subject matter and the principle point of contact.

**Where:** Human Resources careers are found throughout the DHS's agencies.

---

**Who:** Administrative Assistant

**What:** Answers requests and provides advice to employees, supervisors, financial management specialists, and human resource specialists on rules, regulations, and procedures; trains staff on time card issues; works with human resources on pay impacting issues; maintains directories, lists, and other guidelines; sorts and files; transcribes data into documents; and drafts letters and correspondence.

**Where:** Administrative Assistant careers are found throughout the DHS's agencies.

---

**Who:** Engineering Technician

**What:** Monitors and inspects construction contracts, interpreting drawings, specifications, and other contract documents. Investigates and recommend changes in design, specifications, and schedules; reviews contractor's work; performs field inspections; and obtains information for future projects.

**Where:** Engineering Technician careers are found throughout the DHS's agencies.

---

**Who:** General Attorney

**What:** Practices mediation, negotiation, facilitation, conflict coaching, training, and team building; reviews settlements and organizational problems.

**Where:** General Attorneys are employed throughout the DHS's agencies.

---

**Who:** Mission Support Specialist

**What:** Performs a wide variety of administrative and management services essential to the operations of the office, including management and information systems, telecommunications, budget, finance, procurement, human resources, training, logistics, property space, records and files, printing and graphics, mail, travel, and office equipment. Also conducts evaluation of administrative programs, systems, and methods, and identifies ways to improve efficiency and effectiveness.

**Where:** Mission Support Specialist careers are found throughout the DHS's agencies.

---

**Who:** Program Manager

**What:** Manages one or more agency programs determining goals and objectives that need emphasis, develops measures that evaluate performance, makes recommendations for program improvement, manages resources, and assesses implementation by subordinate organizations and operating units. Also identifies and resolves issues where no policy exists, taking innovative actions to address new needs and or issues.

**Where:** Program Manager careers are found throughout the DHS's agencies.

---

**Who:** Lead Program Analyst

**What:** Coordinates, coaches, facilitates, and consensus-builds with federal and contractor analytical teams. Articulates and communicates group assignments, projects, actionable events, milestones, and program issues under review. Monitors and reports status of work and conveys findings and recommendations to management.

**Where:** Lead Program Analyst careers are found throughout the DHS's agencies.

**Who:** General Biological Scientist

**What:** Participates in reviews of ongoing research and development projects to assess potentially fruitful areas for new and additional research and developmental capabilities. Also matches customer needs with research and development capabilities of foreign universities, research institutes, and other entities.

**Where:** General Biological Scientists are found primarily within the Directorate of Science and Technology and the U.S. Coast Guard.

**Who:** Investigative Assistant

**What:** Performs administrative and technical assistance to criminal investigators in the area of investigation, protection, counterfeit, asset forfeiture, and financial crimes. Conducts preliminary searches; inputs data into centralized computerized databases to develop background information on subjects of investigation; acts as liaison, shares information, and extends appropriate assistance to local, state, and federal law enforcement agencies or officials.

**Where:** Investigative Assistant careers are found throughout the DHS's agencies.

**Who:** Director of Intelligence

**What:** Is responsible for the collection, analysis, and sharing of information on critical homeland security vulnerabilities that could be exploited by terrorists and criminal organizations. Processes information from a wide variety of sources to provide assessments of patterns, trends, and new developments in a wide variety of law enforcement areas, including human smuggling and trafficking, fraud and document fraud, drug smuggling, terrorism, cyber crimes, security at critical federal facilities and other critical infrastructure sites, airspace security, commercial fraud, arms trafficking, technologies transfer, and air and marine smuggling. Provides leadership and direction in the development, coordination, and implementation of intelligence programs and operations.

**Where:** Director of Intelligence careers are found throughout the DHS's agencies.

**Who:** Forensics Auditor

**What:** Plans, performs, and advises on a variety of external audit assignments in connection with financial and/or site enforcement audits of suspected criminal organizations and businesses. Provides technical assistance and analysis to criminal investigators and others as required in the course of an investigation utilizing a variety of audit procedures, statistical techniques, and data analysis to assemble and develop findings.

**Where:** Forensics Auditors are found throughout the DHS's agencies.

**Who:** Accountant

**What:** Provides advice and guidance on accounting concepts and principles, including financial reporting, internal audits, accounting operations, budget procedures, formal reviews, systems relationship with financial management, and generally accepted accounting principles. Performs technical accounting assignments; establishes documents to coordinate and execute the internal control activities, assessments, and assurances.

**Where:** Accountant careers are found throughout the DHS's agencies.

**Who:** Safety and Occupational Health Manager

**What:** Serves as agency representative and technical resource for the development and review of occupational safety and health programs. Serves as a technical specialist in a wide variety of operations including disaster response and recovery, materials handling, electrical systems, fire prevention and emergency plans, job hazard analysis, employee training, safety programs, facility inspections, ergonomics, and air quality. Also investigates work-related injuries, and participates in disaster planning and exercises and meetings.

**Where:** Safety and Occupational Health Manager careers are found throughout the DHS's agencies.

**Who:** Contract Specialist

**What:** Is responsible for the acquisition of equipment and services, including solicitations, negotiation, administration, close-out and termination of purchase orders and contracts. Responsible for commodities including furniture, telecommunication equipment, ammunition, surveillance equipment, information technology support services, and guard services. Also responsible for providing technical advice, guidance, and legal interpretation in all areas of contracting, including developing, implementing, and reviewing contracts for pre-award and post-award price/cost analysis.

**Where:** Contract Specialists are found throughout the DHS's agencies.

**Who:** Security Specialist

**What:** Coordinates national programs and develops national capabilities to prevent improvised explosive device (IED) attacks against key resources by performing vulnerability identification, risk analysis, assessment of evolving threats, security evaluations, developing and coordinating vulnerability reduction measures, and performing preventive and protective action planning and implementation.

**Where:** Security Specialists are found throughout the DHS's agencies.

**Who:** Property Management Specialist

**What:** Applies experience and knowledge of property management, related business principles, concepts, regulations, practices, and analytical methods to perform large work projects. Oversees asset cataloging and entry of data into property management systems, and recommends solutions regarding systems and procedures.

**Where:** Property Management Specialists are found throughout the DHS's agencies.

**Who:** Communication Specialist

**What:** Assesses, develops, implements, and evaluates the effectiveness of communication strategies, materials, and programs, including internal and external websites; plans, researches, writes, and edits publications. Also evaluates information flow issues relating to the Internet.

**Where:** Contract Specialists are found throughout the DHS's agencies.

**Who:** Equal Employment Specialist

**What:** Use a comprehensive knowledge of the federal sector equal employment opportunity principles, regulations, analytical methods, and techniques in addressing and accomplishing strategic objectives related to workforce representation and diversity management. Reviews policies and procedures in order to make recommendations requiring modification and adaptation in cases of law, policy, agency practice, and recent court rulings.

**Where:** Equal Employment Specialists are found throughout the DHS's agencies.

# FUTURE PROSPECTS IN MISSION SUPPORT CAREERS

The United States faces new and complex problems in our global economy. As technology increases, the need for experts to lead the future direction of DHS increases. Since September 11, 2001, we have seen a huge advance in the development of scientific technologies in the application of homeland security. This trend will continue, with a serious need for scientists and engineers to develop the necessary tools to protect the United States from its enemies.

The information technologies field in the United States is growing exponentially. The need for career professionals with cybersecurity expertise, program development ability, and research technologies capabilities is found in DHS. The Department of Homeland Security leads the United States in protecting the nation's critical infrastructure and the trend will continue to grow.

The field of safety and health has become the focus of a major push in the United States to protect its citizens from terrorists, major accidents, and national disasters. The Department of Homeland Security needs people who can lead in the planning, prevention, and treatment of problems that could affect the nation as a whole, as well as during a time of crisis. The future of the government's role in safety and protection in the medical, scientific research, and planning creates a great need in DHS.

Do not forget the role played by the support staff in each of the DHS departments. Without a support staff maintaining records, processing the research, and even answering the phones, the effectiveness of operations within DHS would cease to exist.

In the next chapter, we will look at the careers in DHS that most people know about, because, especially while traveling, they encounter people in the law enforcement careers found in DHS.

# CHAPTER three

## LAW ENFORCEMENT CAREERS

**CAREERS IN** law enforcement comprise one of the largest occupations in DHS. The careers themselves vary greatly, from patrolling the nation's borders and waterways, enforcing laws, to maintaining order and investigating crimes. In this chapter we look at the four major law enforcement departments in DHS and some of the exciting careers they offer:

- ▶ United States Secret Service
- ▶ United States Customs and Border Protection (CBP)
- ▶ United States Immigration and Customs Enforcement (ICE)
- ▶ Federal Law Enforcement Training Center (FLETC)

Another major DHS law enforcement path not discussed in this chapter, the Federal Air Marshal Service, is covered in detail in the following chapter.

## UNITED STATES SECRET SERVICE

The United States Secret Service (USSS) is known as one of the most elite law enforcement organizations in the world. The agency has over 4,500 law enforcement career positions and has more than 140 years of service to the United States. Their mission is as follows:

> *The mission of the United States Secret Service is to safeguard the nation's financial infrastructure and payment systems to preserve the integrity of the economy, and to protect national leaders, visiting heads of state and government, designated sites and national security events.*

### QUICK FACT

The United States Secret Service not only protects the president but also safeguards the nation's financial infrastructure.

## Secret Service Uniformed Division

The Secret Service Uniformed Division (USSS-UD) was established in 1922 as the White House Police Force and was integrated into the Secret Service in 1930. Today under the Uniformed Division, there are more than 1,300 officers.

### CAREER SNAPSHOT

**Who:**   Secret Service Uniformed Division Officer

**What:**   Is responsible for security at the White House complex, the vice-presidential residence, the Department of Treasury, and foreign diplomatic missions.

**Where:** Fixed posts as well as foot, bicycle, vehicular, and motorcycle patrols in the Washington, DC area.

**Specializations:**

Countersniper Support Unit (CS), Canine Explosives Detection Unit (K-9), Emergency Response Team (ERT), Magnetometer Support Unit.

## The Secret Service Special Agents Division

The job of a Secret Service Special Agent is to carry out the USSS's twofold mission—safeguard the integrity of the nation's financial system and protect the president and other important figures. Throughout the course of his or her career, a special agent will have assignments in both areas—in the form of field investigations and protection details—and must be willing to travel anywhere in the world.

## CAREER SNAPSHOT

**Who:** Secret Service Special Agent

**What:** *Field Investigation*—investigates counterfeiting crimes, protective intelligence, financial institutions fraud, access-device fraud (such as credit card and debit card fraud), computer crimes, fraudulent government and commercial securities, fictitious financial instruments, telecommunication fraud, false identification, and identity theft. *Protection Detail*—protects the president and others in the line of succession to the office of the president, visiting heads of foreign states or governments, their families, and so forth.

**Where:** *Field Investigation*—over 150 field offices in the United States and abroad; *Protection Detail*—anywhere in the world.

**Specialized Training:**

Criminal law, investigative techniques, combating counterfeiting, combating access-device fraud and other financial criminal activities, protective intelligence investigations, marksmanship, control tactics, water survival skills, physical protection techniques, protective advances, and emergency medicine.

The USSS's dedicated professionalism is observed on the sidelines of the government's most important events. If you think you possess the special qualities needed for employment in the USSS, this elite law enforcement service may hold the challenges you desire in a career.

## UNITED STATES CUSTOMS AND BORDER PROTECTION

U.S. Customs and Border Protection (CBP) is the largest and most complex component of the DHS, with a priority mission of protecting the nation from terrorists, human and drug smuggling, contraband, interdiction of agricultural pests and diseases, revenue and trade, and illegal immigration. CBP law enforcement officers are responsible for guarding nearly 7,000 miles of land border the United States shares with Canada and Mexico and 2,000 miles of coastal waters surrounding the Florida peninsula and off the coast of Southern California. The CBP also protects 95,000 miles of maritime border in partnership with the United States Coast Guard.

The CBP has more than 17,000 CBP Border Patrol agents, 1,000 CBP Air and Marine agents, and almost 22,000 CBP officers and agriculture specialists. The CBP also has the nation's largest law enforcement canine program.[1]

Customs and Border Protection's mission is as follows:

> We are the guardians of our nation's borders.
>
> We are America's frontline.
>
> We safeguard the American homeland.
>
> We protect the American public against terrorists and the instruments of terror.
>
> We steadfastly enforce the laws of the United States while fostering our nation's economic security through lawful international trade and travel.
>
> We serve the American public with vigilance, integrity, and professionalism.[2]

Customs and Border Protection has three law enforcement divisions:

► CBP officers
► Border patrol agents
► Marine interdiction agents

## Customs and Border Protection Officers

The primary responsibility of the CBP officer is the detection of terrorists and weapons of mass destruction and preventing them from entering the United States. He or she must do this while facilitating the orderly flow of legitimate trade and travelers.

### CAREER SNAPSHOT

**Who:**       Customs and Border Protection Officer

**What:**      Enforces a wide variety of laws relating to revenue and trade, seizure of contraband, interdiction of agricultural pests and diseases, and the admissibility of persons.

**Where:**     Over 300 U.S. ports of entry located at seaports, international airports, and land border crossings, focusing on ships, containers, cruise ship passengers, commercial trucking and passenger vehicles.

**Specialized Training:**

Is schooled in antiterrorism; detection of contraband; interviewing; cross-cultural communications; firearms handling and qualification; immigration and naturalization laws; U.S. Customs export and import laws; defensive tactics; arrest techniques; baton techniques; examination of cargo, bags, and merchandise; border search exception; entry and control procedures; passenger processing; officer safety and survival; and advanced technology-based inspection techniques.

## QUICK FACT

Customs and Border Protection officers selected for duty in Puerto Rico, Miami, or along the Southwest border must pass a Spanish-language proficiency exam or successfully complete an additional six weeks of Spanish-language training.

## Border Patrol Agents

Border Patrol Agents are tasked to protect over 6,000 miles of land and 2,000 miles of the coastal United States boundaries from terrorists and illegal entry. With over 11,000 agents, the border patrol is a mobile, uniformed law enforcement division originally established in 1924 in response to illegal immigration into the United States. Since September 11, 2001, however, the focus changed to include the detection and apprehension of terrorists and terrorists' weapons of mass destruction.

## CAREER SNAPSHOT

**Who:**      Border Patrol Agent

**What:**     Detects, prevents, and apprehends terrorists, undocumented aliens, and smugglers of aliens by maintaining surveillance; following leads; responding to electronic sensor television systems; aircraft sightings; and interpreting and following tracks, marks, and other physical evidence. Other major activities include farm and ranch checks; traffic checks and observation; city patrol; transportation checks; administrative, intelligence, and other antismuggling operations.

**Where:**    At or near all U.S. borders; a majority of duties are in rural areas, outdoors, often on foot.

**Specialized Training:**

Is schooled in the use of firearms, advanced physical and driving techniques, nationality and immigration law, as well as applied authority techniques.

If you like working outdoors and find the idea of protecting the nation's home front appealing, a career as a CBP border patrol agent may be right up your alley. For more detailed information, please see *Becoming a Border Patrol Agent*, published by Learning Express, LLC.

## Marine Interdiction Agent

Customs and Border Protection Marine Interdiction Agents (MIA) are an elite group that patrol the nation's oceans, lakes, and rivers. An MIA's mission is to protect the American people and the nation's critical infrastructure through the coordinated use of air and marine forces to detect, interdict, and prevent acts of terrorism and the unlawful movement of people, illegal drugs, and other contraband toward or across the borders of the United States.

**CAREER SNAPSHOT**

**Who:**   Marine Interdiction Agent

**What:**   Command and operate agency vessels to detect, track, and interdict unlawful vessels and personnel, as well as deploy to the scenes of disaster to aid those in need. Agents collect and receive intelligence information and evidence obtained in the marine environment, conduct covert marine operations, prepare investigative reports, and coordinate activities with local, state, and other federal agencies.

**Where:**   Inland waters and coastal territories of the United States; frequently operating at night.

**Specialized Training:**
Marine Law Enforcement Training and boat operators' training.

If you're law-enforcement minded, enjoy being outdoors on the water operating vessels, a career as a Marine Interdiction Agent may be right for you.

## UNITED STATES IMMIGRATION AND CUSTOMS ENFORCEMENT

With over 17,000 employees, United States Immigration and Customs Enforcement (ICE) is the largest investigative arm of DHS. Immigration and Customs Enforcement's mission is to protect national security by enforcing United States customs and immigration laws.

Immigration and Customs Enforcement is comprised of both uniformed and nonuniformed law enforcement positions. Members of ICE conduct investigations into finance and trade, cyber crimes, and project analysis. They litigate removal cases in immigration court and work with foreign authorities conducting intelligence gathering. Immigration and Customs Enforcement investigates arms and strategic technologies violations, human trafficking, and child exploitation. Immigration and Customs Enforcement provides security for federal buildings, crowd control, and surveillance. In addition, ICE members perform the law enforcement duties that include the apprehension, processing, detention, and deportation of illegal or criminal aliens.

The major ICE law enforcement careers available are:

▶ Inspector
▶ Immigration enforcement agent
▶ Technical enforcement/intelligence officer
▶ Federal protective service officers, investigators, and special agents

### CAREER SNAPSHOTS

**Who:**  ICE Inspector

**What:**  Examines immigration applications, visas, and passports. Conducts interviews to determine eligibility for admission, residence, and travel into the United States. Detains people found to be in violation of customs and immigration laws. Inspects cargo, baggage, and personal articles entering and leaving the United States.

**Where:**   All ports of entry into the United States and worldwide.

---

**Who:**   Immigration Enforcement Agent

**What:**   Processes, deports, or escorts aliens who have been ordered to be removed from the United States back to their country of citizenship; detects and exposes identity and benefit fraud; gathers intelligence, evidence, and information to interrogate and debrief aliens in their care.

**Where:**   All ports of entry into the United States and worldwide.

---

**Who:**   Technical Enforcement/Intelligence Officer

**What:**   Collects evidence by planning and executing court-ordered covert surveillance and entries, search warrants, and phone traces for the electronic surveillance phase of major investigative and enforcement actions. May serve on high-risk special operations teams.

**Where:**   Wherever needed.

**Specialized Training:**

Is trained in the use, instruction, maintenance, troubleshooting, and integration of the full range of electronic surveillance devices, including but not limited to telephone, video, audio, tracking, radio frequency technologies, and associated unique surveillance systems.

## Federal Protective Service

The mission of the Federal Protective Service (FPS) is to protect federal properties for federal employees, officials, and visitors in a professional and cost-effective manner by deploying a highly trained and multidisciplined police force comprised of security officers, criminal investigators, inspectors, and police officers.

**QUICK FACT**

Federal Protective Services uniformed officers protect the federal properties of the U.S. government, providing physical security for federal employees, government officials, and visitors.

Federal Protective Service assists the Federal Emergency Management Agency (FEMA) during natural disasters, maintaining control and communications. It also lends itself to special events like national terrorism trials, antiwar protests, Free Trade Area of the Americas summit, World Trade Organization meetings, and the G-8 Summit. They maintain response units consisting of K-9 explosives detector teams, motorcycles, bikes, and hazard and mobile command units. Federal Protective Service also utilizes over 15,000 contract security officers to help in the fight against threats to the U.S. critical infrastructure and employees.

## FEDERAL LAW ENFORCEMENT TRAINING CENTER

The Federal Law Enforcement Training Center (FLETC) is the largest law enforcement training establishment in the country. It is headquartered in Glynco, Georgia and has training facilities in Artesia, New Mexico; Charleston, South Carolina; Cheltenham, Maryland; as well as international facilities.

The center provides basic and specialized training for over 85 federal agencies, as well as state, local, and international police organizations, and assembles the finest professionals from diverse backgrounds to serve on its faculty and staff. Its training programs include:

### Basic Training Programs
▶ Criminal Investigators Training Program
▶ Uniformed Police Training Program
▶ Land Management Training Program

### Advanced Training Programs
▶ Cyber Terrorism Training (Internet forensics and investigation, financial forensics, international banking, and money laundering)
▶ Critical Infrastructure Protection (land transportation antiterrorism, weapons of mass destruction, and seaport security)
▶ Antiterrorism Intelligence Awareness Training (provided for state and local law enforcement agencies)
▶ Marine Law Enforcement Training (for agencies tasked with enforcement on the waters)

In addition, FLETC teaches over 150 other basic and advanced agency-specific training programs.

## Careers at FLETC

The Federal Law Enforcement Training Center is looking for highly experienced instructors to lead the next generation of officers and investigators. Classified as law enforcement specialists, instructors provide practical tactical and technical training in the classroom and field environments. Instructors prepare officers for a multitude of threats by providing training in behavioral sciences, counterterrorism, legal fundamentals, forensic technologies, physical techniques, firearms, and much more. The instructors provide high-quality training to law enforcement officers and investigators from a wide variety of different participating organizations. An instructor assists in the design and development of instructional course materials in the field of law enforcement and uses diverse instructional methods in order to present law enforcement subjects.

The center also looks for retirees from federal law enforcement to reenter the workforce as instructors. If you have specialized law enforcement expertise and the ability and desire to share that knowledge with others, a career as a FLETC law enforcement specialist can be a rewarding career choice on many levels.

## THE DHS LAW ENFORCEMENT PATH

The options discussed in this chapter just scratch the surface of all the law enforcement positions available within DHS. If you're serious about a career in law enforcement, take the time to further investigate all the available career options, and talk with those in the field about their jobs, as discussed in Chapter 13.

# CHAPTER four

## IMMIGRATION AND TRAVEL SECURITY CAREERS

**WHETHER TRAVELING** by airplane, boat, rail, or even subway, you have probably encountered a DHS employee. The immigration and travel careers found within DHS provide an integral service to all people traveling into and out of the United States, as well as from state to state. This chapter discusses careers in the following two departments:

▶ United States Citizenship and Immigration Services (USCIS)
▶ Transportation Security Administration (TSA)

## UNITED STATES CITIZENSHIP AND IMMIGRATION SERVICES

United States Citizenship and Immigration Services (USCIS) controls all lawful immigration into the United States. As part of this mission, USCIS decides on the visa petitions, naturalization petitions, and asylum and refugee petitions of potential immigrants. It oversees citizenship, lawful permanent residency, family and employment related immigration, employment authorization, intercountry adoptions, asylums and refugee status, replacement immigration documents, and foreign student authorization.

An employee of USCIS may process the applications of refugees, adoptions, fiancé(e)s wishing to enter the United States, and employers wishing to bring workers into the country; he or she may swear in new citizens, conduct background checks on potential immigrants, investigate fraud, or fingerprint and photograph applicants for immigration.

### QUICK DEFINITION

Adjudicate (v.): To make a legal judgment upon.

In 2008 alone, USCIS hired an additional 1,700 new employees just to handle the more than half-million immigration filings processed monthly.[1] Let us look at individual jobs found within USCIS. With such a large volume of filings alone, it is not hard to imagine the number of different jobs needed at the USCIS; here are some samples:

### CAREER SNAPSHOTS

**Who:**   Asylum Officer

**What:**   Adjudicates asylum applications; conducts reasonable, credible fear screenings; and adjudicates other benefit applications. Also reviews applications and supporting evidence; conduct interviews; researches information provided by the Office of Refugee, Asylum, and International Operations, the Department of State, and other sources. Interprets and applies appropriate policy, regulations, statutes, and precedent decisions to make eligibility determinations, and produces written assessments supporting decisions.

**Who:**   Immigration Services Officer

**What:**   Acts as the focal point and primary contact for aliens and others seeking information, assistance, and/or guidance in applying for benefits and privileges under the immigration and nationality laws, rules, and regulations. Provides technical and administrative advice to those who examine applications and petitions for immigration benefits, supporting documentation, and related files; and provides information and advisory services to various members of the public, attorneys, and members of Congress.

**Who:**   Immigration Services Analyst

**What:**   Works with adjudication personnel to resolve issues with applications. Verifies data for accuracy, timeliness, and completeness and takes appropriate corrective action; develops briefings and presentations; formulates policy and guidelines; and conducts training and standardization of procedures.

**Who:**   CIS Clerk

**What:**   Evaluates applications and related materials for completeness and consistency in statements, determines whether supporting documentation is sufficient, prepares replies to applicants requesting additional information, and determines and annotates the most appropriate section of the law under which the application of petition can be processed. A CIS clerk must also be able to explain the basic eligibility requirements and provisions of the law to the applicants and interested parties.

**Who:**   Management and Program Analyst

**What:**   Implements, coordinates, and oversees a variety of complex management programs that will impact agency activities. An analyst also plans and conducts special in-depth studies, and develops or makes changes to existing issuances and directives. In addition, determines the applicability and effect of new or proposed legislation, executive orders, agency and bureau directives, and other agency decisions on organization, operations, managerial programs and requirements.

**Who:**    Immigration Officer

**What:**    Performs a variety of fraud detection and national security-related duties consistent with the national effort. Works closely with Immigration and Custom Enforcement, and local, state, and other federal agency personnel to ensure that background checks are conducted on all aliens seeking benefits.

---

**Who:**    Adjudications Officer

**What:**    Oversees the planning and conduct of independent research concerning eligibility entitlements of people seeking immigration benefits, employment, or legal status. Reviews and makes determinations on cases, hears and adjudicates appeals, and decides on motions to reopen and reconsider a case.

---

**Who:**    Operations Support Specialist

**What:**    Provides a variety of management services essential to the operations of USCIS, such as support of human resources functions. Performs management-employee labor relations, training, operations security, procurement activities, and inventories and documents information.

---

**Who:**    Records Manager

**What:**    Coordinates the orderly flow of appropriate files and records between headquarters, on-site managers, the National Records Center, and operational programs, and ensures the appropriate and accurate release of information. Provides technical and administrative supervision to the records section.

---

**Who:**    Business Operations Specialist

**What:**    Provides expert advice and assistance on complex, high-dollar-value contracts for services, systems, and equipment. Consults on identifying program needs and resources, including staffing, funding, equipment, facilities, and delivery of performance schedules for offices.

---

**Who:**    Immigration Services Assistant

**What:**    Manages correspondence, maintains customer support, processes documents and fees, as well as performing analyses on files, reports, and information systems or databases. Also initiates security checks and conducts file searches for aliases, dates of birth, and criminal behavior. Prescreens various applications and submissions by customers for accuracy, completeness of initial supporting documentation, and eligibility for benefits. Educates applicants as to the options available to them and the appropriate applications to file.

Citizenship and Immigration Services is tasked with a vast undertaking of processing all applications and petitions for immigration into the United States, and these examples are by no means a complete listing of careers available within USCIS. If you enjoy working directly with people from diverse cultures and backgrounds and performing investigative searches, or like the idea of managing an office dedicated to protecting the United States from fraud and terrorism, then USCIS may have a position just for you.

## TRANSPORTATION SECURITY ADMINISTRATION

The Transportation Security Administration (TSA) was formed by the federal government immediately following the attacks of September 11, 2001, to protect the nation's transportation systems and ensure the freedom of movement of people and commerce.

As a component of DHS, TSA is responsible for the security at over 450 airports, as well as the nation's highways, railroads, buses, mass transport systems, and ports. It employs over 50,000 as security officers, inspectors, directors, air marshals, and managers.

Let's look at some of largest TSA career opportunities.

### Transportation Security Officers

At over 43,000 strong, transportation security officers (TSOs) make up the largest group of careers available in TSA. A TSO performs a variety of duties related to providing security and protection of air travelers, airports, and aircraft. In the course of a normal day on the job, a TSO may be required to:

- ▶ conduct security screenings of individuals by hand wand, pat-down, and monitoring walk-through metal detectors
- ▶ perform property security screenings with X-ray machines to identify dangerous objects in baggage and cargo, and on passengers
- ▶ monitor the flow of passengers through the screening process to facilitate their orderly and efficient processing
- ▶ control and monitor the entry and exit points of the facilities to which they are deployed.

Once hired, a transportation security officer goes through an intensive 160-hour training program on the latest technology, behavioral recognition, and screening techniques utilized in the job. While employed, he or she is required to receive approximately 22 hours per quarter in ongoing training.

## QUICK FACT

There are approximately 100 transportation security inspectors assigned to 18 field offices across the United States.

## CAREER SNAPSHOTS

**Who:** Transportation Security Inspector (TSI)

**What:** Is responsible for ensuring security compliance of people, freight, and surface transportation systems by performing frequent inspections of key facilities, including stations and terminals, for potential threats. Also evaluates the integration of new technology, traditional security measures, and human factors to ensure the operational effectiveness and efficiency of the overall security system and collects, records, and analyzes data pertaining to the transportation industry.

**Who:** Behavioral Detection Officer (BDO)

**What:** Performs passive observation and engages in voluntary encounters with travelers to determine whether elevated behaviors indicate that the individual may be involved in terrorist or criminal activity. Determines baseline information, which includes identifying flight destinations, understanding the anticipated composition of travelers associated with flights and behaviors expected, and assessing deviations from such behaviors.

**Who:** Bomb Appraisal Officer (BAO)

**What:** Is responsible for all issues involving explosives, improvised explosive devices, and chemical, biological, radiological, and nuclear threats. Responds to and assesses all unresolved checkpoint alarms, contacts appropriate authorities, clears and readies checkpoints for special operations, and determines whether alarms are negative or positive regarding the presence of a potentially destructive device.

**Who:** Special Security Officer

**What:** Is involved in the internal security disciplines required for the daily operation of two to three sensitive compartmented information (SCI) facilities. A special security officer is also responsible for one or more of the following internal security disciplines—personnel security, communication security, physical security, communication security (COMSEC) information security, and information systems security. Conducts background checks, assists with security education, and investigates facility violations.

**Who:** Coordination Center Officer (CCO)

**What:** Performs duties within an airport's coordination center gathering, analyzing, and evaluating data and making risk/threat assessments. Maintains a relationship with all involved in security and airport operations and plans, develops, and coordinates emergency operations during a time of crisis. Also maintains security screening credentials and may be called to fill-in positions.

**Who:** Aviation Regulatory Inspector

**What:** Conducts assessments and investigations of airports and air carriers to determine security posture, identify potential problem areas or deviations from prescribed standards, and provide technical guidance to airports and air carriers on the development or modification of a large number of security plans to ensure compliance with regulatory requirements.

## Federal Air Marshal

Federal air marshals (FAMs) serve as the primary law enforcement entity within TSA under the TSA Office of Law Enforcement. An air marshal detects, deters, and defeats hostile acts targeting U.S. air carriers, airports, passengers, and air crew. An FAM typically does this by operating independently, blending in as an air passenger—spending an average of 181 days a year and approximately five hours of each of those days in flight.

Air marshals work closely with other law enforcement agencies and staff positions with the National Counterterrorism Center and the National Targeting Center, and on the Federal Bureau of Investigation's Joint Terrorism Task Force, and may also be distributed among other law enforcement and DHS agencies during times of heightened alert or special national security. An FAM is trained in investigative techniques, criminal terrorist behavior recognition, firearms proficiency, aircraft-specific tactics, and close-quarters defense. Training consists of a seven-week basic law enforcement course at the Federal Law Enforcement Training Center, followed by additional training at the Federal Aviation Administration's William J. Hughes Technical Center in Atlantic City, New Jersey.

The immigration and travel security careers just listed provide only a glimpse of the possibilities available in this area of the DHS. If any of these careers piqued your interest, you should investigate further using the resources found at the end of this book. You'll discover a wide variety of managerial, directorial, and specialist positions that may suit your skills, aspirations, and personality perfectly.

# CHAPTER five

## PREVENTION AND RESPONSE CAREERS

**THE DHS** defines *prevention* as the security measures taken in order to discourage terrorist acts on the United States through activities, practices, and law enforcement rules and regulations aimed at anticipating, avoiding, and removing possible causes to preclude a hazardous incident. *Response* is the reaction to an occurrence or situation aimed at controlling and containment in the wake of a disaster, whether it is natural or manmade.

In this chapter, we examine prevention and response careers within DHS and specifically, the two agencies that deal with the prevention of and response to issues that face the United States.

▶ United States Coast Guard
▶ Federal Emergency Management Agency

## THE UNITED STATES COAST GUARD

The United States Coast Guard (USCG) is a military organization that serves under DHS with roles in maritime homeland security, maritime law enforcement, search and rescue, marine environmental protection, and the maintenance of river, intracoastal, and offshore aids to navigation. The Coast Guard is comprised of approximately 42,000 active duty enlisted personnel and officers, 7,659 civilians, and 7,484 reserve personnel.[1]

The Coast Guard has 11 missions under DHS, listed here in order of importance:

### Mission 1: Ports, Waterways, and Coastal Security

Protect the United States, its transportation system, ports, waterways, and coast from terrorist acts, sabotage, espionage, or subversive acts, and respond to and assist in recovery from those that do occur.

### Mission 2: Drug Interdiction

Reduce the supply of drugs from the source by denying smugglers the use of air and maritime routes into the United States. The Coast Guard is the lead federal agency for maritime drug interdiction and shares the lead responsibility for air interdiction with the Customs and Border Protection's air interdiction units.

### Mission 3: Maintain Aids to Navigation

Maintain the Aids to Navigation System to promote safe vessel navigation on the waters of the United States and its territories.

### Mission 4: Search and Rescue

Render aid to people in distress to minimize loss of life, injury, or property damage. The USCG search and rescue response involves multimission stations, cutters, aircraft, and boats ready at a moment's notice 24/7, 365 days a year, to rescue people in trouble on the water.

## Mission 5: Living Marine Resources

Ensure the United States' marine-protected species are provided the protection necessary to maintain sustainable, healthy levels by patrolling the United States Exclusive Zone and enforcing domestic fisheries law and international fisheries agreements.

## Mission 6: Marine Safety

Develop and maintain policy, standards, training, and certification programs to ensure the operators, boats, and ships on the waterways of the United States are safe.

## Mission 7: Defense Readiness

The Coast Guard is a United States armed force serving as a specialized service under the Department of the Navy during a time of war or when directed by the president. The Coast Guard is also responsible for countering threats to America's coasts, ports, and inland waterways through numerous port security, harbor defense, and coastal warfare operations and exercises.

## Mission 8: Migrant Interdiction

Enforce immigration laws at sea. The Coast Guard conducts patrols and coordinates with other federal agencies and foreign countries to interdict undocumented migrants at sea, denying them entry by maritime routes to the United States, its territories, and possessions.

## Mission 9: Marine Environmental Protection

Develop and enforce regulations to stop unauthorized ocean dumping, preventing oil and chemical spills, and avert the introduction of invasive species into the maritime environment.

## Mission 10: Ice Operations

Conduct ice-breaking services to assist vessels and communities in emergency situations and facilitate essential commercial maritime activities on the Great Lakes and Northeast regions. The Coast Guard facilitates scientific research studies in cooperation with other federal agencies in the study of the polar regions of the world and is capable of providing year-round access to those regions. The Coast Guard also maintains the international ice patrol, broadcasting the positions of icebergs to assist the safe navigation of commercial vessels.

## Mission 11: Other Law Enforcement

Protect the Exclusive Economic Zone—the area from land out 200 miles to sea—from foreign encroachment and through international agreements. The Coast Guard acts as the first line of defense in the detection of illegal activities within the zone.

### QUICK FACT

The United States Coast Guard is one of the five branches of the military, but falls under the DHS umbrella because of its role in protection and response. However, during wartime, the USCG may be transferred to the command of the United States Navy.

The United States Coast Guard has a long history of stepping up in times of crisis, always in an effort to protect the United States' maritime interests. The Coast Guard offers career opportunities both on the water and in the air, in search and rescue, scientific research, law enforcement, and maritime safety. Personnel may serve as an officer, as enlisted, or as a civilian. Let us look into specific careers found within the United States Coast Guard.

## MILITARY CAREERS IN THE UNITED STATES COAST GUARD

There are two major military career paths in the USCG—enlisted personnel and officers. Both sign up for a required period of time called a commission or enlistment period, which usually lasts from four to six years. As with the other branches of the military, the Coast Guard offers a retirement program after 20 years of service for both officers and enlisted personnel.

### Officer Career Fields

Although the Coast Guard is the smallest of the nation's military services, it gives big responsibilities to its officers. A commissioned officer can choose career paths in the following career areas:

- ▶ law
- ▶ environmental
- ▶ aviation
- ▶ engineering
- ▶ command, control, and communications
- ▶ computer and information technologies
- ▶ intelligence

### Becoming an Officer

The USCG offers officer candidates the following seven options to become an officer depending on your current education, experience, and training.

### The Coast Guard Academy

Located in New London, Connecticut, the United States Coast Guard Academy is a four-year accredited college program that enrolls approximately 300 cadets annually. Graduates of the academy earn a four-year Bachelor of Science degree and are commissioned in the United States Coast Guard as ensigns. The academy education is free, and cadets earn a modest paycheck during their education period. A graduate must serve for a minimum of five years after graduation.

### Officer Candidate School

Officer Candidate School (OCS) is a 17-week indoctrination into the military lifestyle and the wide range of technical information necessary for performing the duties of an officer in the USCG. Upon successful completion of the training program, graduates receive a commission as ensigns and are required to serve a minimum of three years of active duty. Graduates may be assigned to a ship, flight training, a staff job, or an operations shore billet.

### College Student Pre-Commissioning Initiative Program

This program provides full payment of tuition, fees, textbooks, salary, medical insurance, and other benefits during a student's junior and senior years of college in exchange for three years of service as a commissioned officer. Within 24 months of graduation from college, a student attends Officer Candidate School (OCS) and is commissioned as an ensign.

### Pre-Commissioning Program for Enlisted Personnel

This program allows selected enlisted personnel to attend a college full time for one or two years to meet the commissioned officers degree requirement; they pay for tuition, books, and lab fees, while still receiving full pay and benefits at their enlisted grade. Upon college graduation, they attend Officer Candidate School for 17 weeks and receive a commission as an ensign, and will be required to serve for three years of service in the Coast Guard.

### Direct Commission Programs

These programs provide private-sector professionals a direct route to being commissioned in the Coast Guard without attending Officer Candidate

School. Attorneys, aviators, engineers, environmental specialists, maritime academy graduates, and former military officers who meet the necessary requirements can become an officer in the Coast Guard. Qualified enlistees must attend a three- to five-week resident training program to indoctrinate them into policies of the Coast Guard, and commit to a minimum of three years of service.

### Maritime Academy Graduate Program

This program is available to individuals who hold a degree from a qualifying state or federal maritime academy and hold a third mate or third assistant engineering license, or a degree in marine environmental protection or a related field of study. Upon successful completion, graduates will be commissioned as a lieutenant junior grade or ensign for three years of required service.

### Blue 21 Flight Initiative

The Blue 21 Flight Initiative provides successful graduates of OCS the guaranteed opportunity to attend flight training school in Pensacola, Florida, to become a Coast Guard aviator. Upon completing the flight training, the candidate will be required to serve as an officer for 11 years. If a candidate is unable to complete that flight training, his or her obligation would be the same as that of a graduate of Officer Candidate School—just three years of service.

## Enlisted Personnel Jobs

Enlisted personnel are the backbone of the Coast Guard, providing the manpower to conduct the daily operations of the USCG's multiple missions. Enlisted candidates attend military basic training—boot camp—at the Coast Guard Training Center in Cape May, New Jersey, for a period of eight weeks, where they learn about a variety of subjects including the Uniform Code of Military Justice, Coast Guard history, firefighting, weapons handling, survival equipment and training, as well as physical fitness.

## Becoming an Enlisted

A career as enlisted personnel in the Coast Guard does not require advanced education or training. A candidate will learn on the job and/or attend advanced training classes in the field of his or her choice. The available careers are broken into four categories:

- ▶ deck and ordinance group
- ▶ hull and engineering group
- ▶ aviation group
- ▶ administrative and scientific group

The Coast Guard's enlisted program provides an opportunity for the individual who has not yet had the life experiences that may be required in other careers. Following is a summary, by group, of job opportunities available for enlisted personnel in the USCG.

## CAREER SNAPSHOTS—DECK AND ORDINANCE GROUP

**Who:**      Boatswain's Mate (BM)

**What:**     Performs tasks in connection with deck maintenance, small boat operations, navigation, and supervising all personnel assigned to a ship's deck force. Serves as officer-in-charge of many of the Coast Guard's patrol boats, tugs, small craft, and shore stations and also acts as law enforcement officer in the marine environment, enforcing laws and regulations.

**Training:** Twelve weeks of intensive training at the Coast Guard Training Center in Yorktown, Virginia, or on the job through a striker program. A BM can go on to advanced training as a coxswain, heavy weather coxswain, aids to navigation basic and advanced, buoy deck supervisor, and law enforcement training.

**Who:** Gunner's Mate (GM)

**What:** Is responsible for the training of personnel in the proper handling of weapons, ammunition (everything from pistols, rifles, and machine guns to 76mm weapon systems), and pyrotechnics. Involved with law enforcement and security at marine safety offices and on marine safety teams.

**Training:** Ten weeks of formal instruction in electronics, mechanical systems and hydraulics, and maintenance on all ordinance/gunnery equipment at the Coast Guard Training Center in Yorktown, Virginia. Must also attend specialized equipment/system schools for a period of five to 14 weeks.

---

**Who:** Operations Specialist (OS)

**What:** Performs functions ranging from search and rescue and law enforcement operations to combat information center operations. An operations specialist operates most of the advanced computer systems the Coast Guard has, incorporating satellite communication, global positioning navigation, electronic charting systems to real-time target acquisition, tracking and identification of subjects.

**Training:** Extensive training in search and rescue planning system programs and tools, navigation, and communication.

---

**Who:** Intelligence Specialist (IS)

**What:** Identifies and produces intelligence from raw information; assembles and analyzes multisource operational intelligence, collects and analyzes communication signals using sophisticated computer technology.

**Training:** Ten weeks of specialized training at the Coast Guard Training Center in Yorktown, Virginia.

## CAREER SNAPSHOTS—HULL AND ENGINEERING GROUP

**Who:** Damage Controlman (DC)

**What:** Is responsible for watertight integrity; the emergency equipment associated with firefighting and flooding; plumbing repairs; welding fabrication and repairs; as well as chemical, biological, and nuclear detection; and contamination in Coast Guard systems.

**Training:** Thirteen weeks at the Coast Guard Training Center in Yorktown, Virginia, to learn welding, oxy-fuel gas cutting, firefighting, carpentry, plumbing, watertight closure maintenance, chemical, biological and nuclear defense, and shipboard damage control.

**Who:** Electrician's Mate (EM)

**What:** Is responsible for electrical power generation, fractional and integral horsepower motors, cutter propulsion control, interior communication systems, electronic navigation equipment, and gyrocompass equipment and performing the installation, maintenance, repair, and management of sophisticated electrical and electronic equipment.

**Training:** Intensive training at the Coast Guard Training Center in Yorktown, Virginia, in mathematics, physics, electrical circuit analysis, test equipment, motors, generators, and transformers theory. May also attend courses in advanced analog electronics, digital electronics, programmable logic controllers, and fiber optics.

**Who:** Electronics Technician (ET)

**What:** Is responsible for the installation, maintenance, repair, and management of sophisticated electronics equipment, such as command and control systems, shipboard weapons, and the guidance and fire-control systems. ETs are also responsible for communications receivers and transmitters, data and voice encryption equipment, navigation and search radar, tactical and electronic detection systems, and electronic navigation equipment and navigational computers.

**Training:** Attends a 28-week training program at the Coast Guard Training Center in Petaluma, California, and may receive additional specialized training.

**Who:** Information Systems Technician (IT)

**What:** Is responsible for establishing and maintaining Coast Guard computer systems, analog and digital voice systems, and installing and maintaining the physical network infrastructure. Information systems technicians also perform work on servers and workstations, install copper and fiber-optic cable, and will learn adds, moves, branches, and changes on private branch exchange and electronic key telephone systems.

**Training:** Twenty-five weeks of training at the Coast Guard Training Center in Petaluma, California, and instruction on installing the standard computer systems utilized by the Coast Guard.

**Who:** Machinery Technician (MT)

**What:** Is responsible for all areas of machinery operation and maintenance from internal combustion engines to environmental support systems. Machinery technicians are also called upon to act as law enforcement officers in the Coast Guard.

**Training:** Twelve weeks of instruction in Yorktown, Virginia, or qualification through on-the-job training.

## CAREER SNAPSHOTS—AVIATION GROUP

**Who:** Avionics Electrical Technician (AET)

**What:** Inspects, maintains, troubleshoots, and repairs avionics systems that perform communications, navigation, collision avoidance, target acquisition, and automatic flight control. Also inspects, maintains, troubleshoots, and repairs aircraft batteries, AC and DC power generation, conversion, and distribution systems servicing USCG aircraft. Serves as part of the air crew in flight.

**Training:** Twenty weeks at the Aviation Training Center in Elizabeth City, North Carolina, covering basic aviation and electrical maintenance fundamentals.

**Who:** Aviation Maintenance Technician (AMT)

**What:** Ground handling and servicing of aircraft, conducting routine aircraft inspections, and performing administrative duties. Also repairs aircraft engines, auxiliary power units, props, rotor systems, power train systems, and associated airframe, fuselage, wings, and moveable flight control systems.

**Training:** Sixteen weeks of on-the-job training followed by a commanding officer's recommendation, then 20 weeks of specialized classroom training at the Aviation Training Center in Elizabeth City, North Carolina.

**Who:**  Aviation Survival Technician (AST)

**What:**  Serves as the air crew rescue swimmer, performing air-sea rescues and lifesaving duties. Also inspects, services, maintains, repairs, and troubleshoots cargo aerial delivery systems, drag parachute systems, aircraft oxygen systems, dewatering pumps, and survival equipment.

**Training:**  Sixteen weeks of physically demanding specialized training at the Aviation Training Center in Elizabeth City, North Carolina, followed by three weeks of emergency medical training (EMT) located at the Coast Guard Training Center, Petaluma, California.

## CAREER SNAPSHOTS—ADMINISTRATIVE AND SCIENTIFIC GROUP

**Who:**  Food Service Specialist (FS)

**What:**  Is responsible for the food preparation, accounting, and management of USCG galleys, both aboard ships and at shore stations. A food service specialist may service a large kitchen serving thousands of meals, or small galleys serving a small crew.

**Training:**  Twelve weeks of specialized food preparation study at the Coast Guard Training Center in Petaluma, California, or on-the-job training.

---

**Who:**  Health Services Technician (HS)

**What:**  Provides direct medical care and assists medical and dental officers with X-rays, diagnostic testing, clinical lab testing, prescribing medications, administering immunizations, and performing minor surgical procedures.

**Training:**  Thirteen weeks at the Coast Guard Training Center in Petaluma, California, studying anatomy, physiology, patient examination, evaluation, treatment, and pharmacology.

---

**Who:**  Marine Science Technician (MST)

**What:**  Conducts marine safety activities, investigates pollution incidents, monitors cleanup efforts, protects the United States from aquatic nuisance species, and examines cargo and passenger ships for compliance with applicable laws and regulations.

**Training:** Nine weeks of training at the Coast Guard Training Center in Yorktown, Virginia, on pollution investigation, pollution response, occupational safety and health, facility inspections, and vessel boarding.

**Who:** Public Affairs Specialist (PA)

**What:** Writes news releases and feature articles, shoots still and video imagery, serves as a spokesperson, and maintains websites to raise public awareness of important Coast Guard issues and news stories.

**Training:** Twelve weeks at the Defense Information School in Ft. Meade, Maryland, learning media relations, journalism, web design, photography, videography, public speaking, and editing and design.

**Who:** Storekeeper (SK)

**What:** Handles all logistic functions of procurement, storage, preservation, packing, and issuance of clothing, spare parts, provisions, technical items, and all other necessary supplies utilized by the Coast Guard.

**Training:** Seven weeks of specialized instruction at the Coast Guard Training Center in Petaluma, California, in requisitioning of supplies and services, property management, materials shipping and receiving, inventory management, financial data entry, and maintenance of financial records.

**Who:** Yeoman (YN)

**What:** Is responsible for the administration of the Coast Guard's units, serving as a human resources personnel manager and administrative specialist. Responsibilities include payroll, travel, scheduling, information source, personnel issues, and the transferring in and out of personnel from a unit.

**Training:** Six-week program in administration, computations, pay and personnel, expiration of enlistment, travel and transportation, and reserves at the Coast Guard Training Center, Petaluma, California, or on-the-job training.

## CIVILIAN CAREERS IN THE UNITED STATES COAST GUARD

Civilians employed by the Coast Guard are just that—civilians—and do not have to enlist for employment, or even know how to swim for that matter!

There are over 200 civilian positions in the USCG, spread across five broad occupational areas:

▶ professional
▶ administrative
▶ technical
▶ trades and labor
▶ administrative support

## QUICK FACT

There are well over 7,000 civilian personnel employed by the United States Coast Guard, and that number continues to grow.

The **professional careers** in the USCG typically require advanced degrees. These careers can be found in the areas of:

| | | |
|---|---|---|
| accounting | educational training | mechanical engineering |
| architecture | vocational training | family advocacy |
| civil engineering | electronics engineering | family child care |
| contracting | law | employee assistance |
| procurement | general engineering | wellness |

**Administrative careers** in the USCG typically involve preparing, receiving, reviewing, and verifying documents; processing transactions; locating and compiling data or other information from various sources; and using a variety of computer products to prepare printed material or to store or manipulate information.

| | | |
|---|---|---|
| administrative specialist | marine inspector | human resources |
| intelligence analyst | commercial fishing industry vessel examiner | safety and occupational health |
| security specialist | housing management specialist | search and rescue controller |
| paralegal specialist | information technology specialist | vessel traffic management |
| budget analyst | | marine transportation specialist |
| criminal investigator | inventory management, logistics management | |
| environmental protection specialist | | |

**Technical careers** in the USCG involve supporting personnel in their professional and administrative occupations. Technicians apply a practical knowledge of principles, concepts, and practices that drive the field of technology. Technical careers include but are not limited to:

engineering technician    construction representative    dental assistant

USCG civilian careers in **trades and labor** include, but are not limited to, the following:

| | | |
|---|---|---|
| aircraft mechanic | maintenance | materials handler |
| electrician | mechanic | painter |
| electronics | marine machinery | sheet metal mechanic |
| mechanic | mechanic | welder |

USCG civilian careers in **administrative support** involve supporting management; preparing, receiving, reviewing, and verifying documents; and processing transactions. Administrative support careers include, but are not limited to:

| | |
|---|---|
| administrative assistant | office automation clerk |
| human resources assistant | procurement assistant |
| housing management assistant | purchasing agent |
| legal assistant | secretary |
| legal instruments examiner | |

Coast Guard civilian employees work in more than 100 locations throughout the United States.


# FEDERAL EMERGENCY MANAGEMENT AGENCY

The Federal Emergency Management Agency (FEMA) is the preeminent emergency management and preparedness agency for the United States. The agency's mandate is to reduce the loss of life and property and protect the United States from hazards, including natural disasters, acts of terrorism, and other man-made disasters by leading and supporting the nation in a risk-based, comprehensive emergency management system of preparedness, protection, response, recovery and mitigation. FEMA's challenge and commitment is to achieve its vision and fully execute the mission to create a safer and more secure America.

## QUICK FACT

The Federal Emergency Management Agency currently has more than 3,700 employees at the ready throughout the United States.

The agency is headquartered in Washington, DC, with ten regional offices throughout the United States, along with the Mount Weather Emergency Operations Center located in Virginia, the national emergency training center in Maryland, and National Processing Centers located in Maryland, Texas, and Virginia. With added responsibilities and directives, in 2007 FEMA began to strengthen its workforce with congressional approval of new full-time positions, a significant number of which were added at the regional level. The agency is working to "develop a nationwide system of trained and certified experts and planners, skilled in all-hazards emergency management, to increase its readiness to meet the range of challenges posed by any disaster."[2]

FEMA offers a wide range of opportunities for people from all walks of life. But if you're the type of person who thrives on being part of the action or a planner who looks into the future to prepare for disasters, FEMA definitely has a place for you.

Though by no means a complete listing, the following is a good sample of the types of careers available in FEMA.

## CAREER SNAPSHOTS

**Who:** Emergency Management Program Specialist

**What:** Ensures that there are adequate operational facilities, staff, and communications for effective and efficient program delivery and support for assigned public assistance disaster declarations.

**Who:** Environmental Protection Specialist

**What:** Plans, coordinates, and evaluates a broad scope of studies and investigations of complex problems related to scientific assessments and risk determinations. Assists with environmental and historic preservation reviews, regulatory consultations, compliance, public outreach, and technical assistance for the Hazard Mitigation Grant Program, Pre-Disaster Mitigation, Flood Mitigation and Assistance, Repetitive Flood Claims, Severe Repetitive Loss, and other program projects and disaster declarations.

**Who:** Fire Program Specialist

**What:** Serves as a FEMA spokesperson on all fire programs and related matters. Is responsible for a variety of program planning, implementation, monitoring, and analysis activities to provide direct assistance to organizations that lack the tools and resources necessary to more effectively protect the health and safety of the public and their emergency response personnel with respect to fire and all other hazards.

**Who:** Contract Specialist

**What:** Coordinates and manages a variety of complex and typically long-term contracts and interagency agreements, entailing the coordination of efforts and the resolution of conflicting and controversial high-profile issues with a number of parties both within and outside DHS/FEMA.

**Who:** Procurement Analyst

**What:** Analyzes management techniques, processes, and styles for improving FEMA's effectiveness. A procurement analyst develops policy; implements regulations and standards on acquisition related programs, activities, and functions; investigates and analyzes trends and conditions; and initiates corrective action.

**Who:** Reports Specialist

**What:** Extracts, compiles, assembles, and classifies statistical data from source materials; computes statistical data for the preparation of unique ad-hoc reports for customers such as FEMA Regional Offices, other governmental agencies, voluntary agencies, and FEMA Headquarters, in support of federal and state disaster recovery programs.

**Who:**     Deployment Specialist

**What:**    Deploys to disaster sites and field offices to perform liaison functions
             on behalf of the Disaster Reserve Workforce Division, including the
             preparation of onsite delivery, the initiation of the staffing station,
             onsite training and mentoring of local staff, and the coordination of
             reporting and staffing requirements for the supported theater.

If a career in prevention or response appeals to you, the Coast Guard or
FEMA may have the job you are looking for. Take the time investigate all
the available career options, and be sure to read Chapter 10 for valuable information on applying.

# CHAPTER six

## CUTTING-EDGE CAREERS IN CYBER SECURITY

## A NEW VULNERABILITY

When the United States first realized that it was vulnerable to aircraft and missiles in the 1950s and 1960s, the federal government quickly responded by creating a national system to monitor the airspace with radar to detect, analyze, and warn of possible attacks; coordinate fighter aircraft defenses during an attack; and restore the nation after an attack through civil defense programs. Today, the United States' critical assets are once again vulnerable to attack, but in a vast, uncharted territory—cyberspace.

### QUICK DEFINITION:

*Cyberspace (n):* The electronic medium of interconnected computer networks, in which online communication takes place.

The information technology revolution changed the way businesses and governments operate. Today, the central nervous system of the nation's critical infrastructure—agriculture, food and water supplies, public health, emergency services, government, defense, industrial base, information and communications, energy, transportation, banking and finance, chemicals and hazardous materials, and postal and shipping—is based in cyberspace.

For example, the United States' power grid is monitored and controlled with the use of computer networks called supervisory control and data acquisition (SCADA). Computer networks also control electrical transformers, pipeline pumps, chemical vats, radar, and other critical systems. It is not hard to imagine what the impact of a terrorist attack on this infrastructure would cause, and though infiltrating our borders to coordinate a physical attack upon these assets may be next to impossible, the medium of cyberspace provides a means for organized attacks on the United States' infrastructure from a distance.

## QUICK FACT

Barack Obama has stated that cyber security is a top priority in his administration. The Department of Homeland Security is the lead agency in the area of cyber security for the United States.

## DEFENDING CYBERSPACE

Countering cyber attacks requires the development of new, cutting-edge capabilities, and the Department of Homeland Security is tasked with the responsibility of securing cyberspace. This responsibility includes:

▶ developing a comprehensive national plan for securing the key resources and critical infrastructure of the United States

▶ providing crisis management in response to an attack on critical information systems

▶ providing technical assistance to the private sector and other government entities with respect to emergency recovery plans for failures of critical information systems

▶ coordinating with other agencies of the federal government to provide specific warning information and advice about appropriate protective measures and countermeasures to state, local, and nongovernmental organizations including the private sector, academia, and the public

▶ performing and funding research and development along with other agencies that will lead to new scientific understanding and technologies in support of homeland security

▶ becoming a federal center of excellence for cyber security and providing a focal point for federal outreach to state, local, and nongovernmental organizations including the private sector, academia, and the public

This new field has provided a unique opportunity for creative and innovative individuals with an interest in creating the cyber technology of tomorrow, while protecting vital infrastructure of the United States. Understanding the various components that make up DHS's cyber security responsibilities can help you in your effort to ascertain where your skills and abilities would be best utilized. Following are the major offices, divisions, and programs found in cyber security within DHS.

## Office of Cybersecurity and Communications

The Office of Cybersecurity and Communications works to prevent or minimize disruptions to the critical information infrastructure in order to protect the public, economy, government services, and the overall security of the United States. It does this through continuous efforts designed to further safeguard federal government systems by reducing potential vulnerabilities, protecting against cyber intrusions, and anticipating future threats. The Office of Cybersecurity and Communications actively engages the public and private sectors, as well as international partners to prepare, prevent, and respond to catastrophic cyber incidents.

## National Cybersecurity Division

The National Cybersecurity Division (NCSD) works collectively with public, private and international entities to secure cyberspace and American cyber assets. The goal of the NCSD is to build and maintain an effective national cyberspace response system and implement a cyber risk management program for the protection of critical infrastructure. It is structured to function through the following programs:

▶ The **Cybersecurity Preparedness and National Cyber Alert System** provides both technical and nontechnical computer users with current information on the latest threats to cyberspace.

▶ The **United States Computer Emergency Readiness Team— US-CERT Operations**—is responsible for analyzing and reducing cyber threats and vulnerabilities, disseminating cyber threat warning information, and coordinating incident response activities.

▶ The **Cyber Cop Portal** coordinates with law enforcement agencies to help capture and convict those responsible for cyber attacks. It is an information sharing and collaboration tool accessed by over 5,300 investigators worldwide involved in electronic crimes cases.

## Cyber Security Research and Development Center

The Cyber Security Research and Development Center (CSRDC) was established by DHS to develop cyber security technology. The center conducts its work through partnerships between government and private industry, the venture capital community, and the research community. It conducts experimental research, Internet route monitoring, experiments and exercises, and is a research data repository. The end users of these research tools include cyber security researchers, developers, and operators. The center is working on the cutting edge of future technology for government as well as the private sector.

## DO YOU HAVE WHAT IT TAKES TO WORK IN DHS CYBER SECURITY?

In response to the need for well-trained, well-equipped information technology security specialists, the Office of Cybersecurity and Communications has developed a document called *Information Technology Security Essential Body of Knowledge (EBK) Competency and Functional Framework for Informational Technology Security Workforce Development.*[1] This document outlines the essential knowledge and skills information technology security practitioners should possess to perform in their field. It is updated every two years and clarifies key information technology security terms and concepts and identifies generic security roles for information technology security specialists. This document provides an IT professional interested in working for DHS the opportunity to match his or her competencies with a role as an information technology security professional with DHS. The *Information Technology Security Essential Body of Knowledge (EBK) Competency and Functional Framework for Informational Technology Security Workforce Development* can be found online at http://www.us-cert.gov/ITSecurityEBK/.

## Career Areas

The DHS is currently looking for individuals with the skills or competencies to work in the following areas:

**Data Security**—the application of principles, policies, and procedures necessary to ensure the confidentiality, integrity, availability, and privacy of data in all forms of media

**Digital Forensics**—the knowledge and understanding of digital investigations and analysis used for acquiring, validating, and analyzing electronic data to reconstruct events related to security incidents

**Enterprise Continuity**—the application of the principles, policies, and procedures that ensure that an enterprise continues to perform essential business functions after the occurrence of a catastrophic event

**Incident Management**—the knowledge and understanding of the process to prepare and prevent, detect, contain, and recover, and the ability to apply lessons learned from incidents impacting the mission of an organization

**Information Technology Training and Awareness**—the principles, practices, and methods required to raise employee awareness about basic information security and train individuals with information security roles to increase their knowledge, skills, and abilities

**Information Technology Systems Operations and Maintenance**— the ongoing application of principles, policies, and procedures to

maintain, monitor, control, and protect information technology infrastructure and the information residing on it during the operations phase
of an information technology system or application in production

**Network and Telecommunications Security**—the application of the
principles, policies, and procedures involved with ensuring the security
of basic network and telecommunications services and data, and in maintaining the hardware layer on which it resides. Examples include perime-
ter defense strategies, defense in depth strategies, and data encryption
techniques.

**Personnel Security**—the methods and controls used to ensure that in
an organization's selection and application of human resources, both
employee and contractor are controlled to promote security. Personnel
security controls are used to prevent and detect employee-caused
security breaches such as, theft, fraud, misuse of information, and
noncompliance.

**Physical and Environmental Security**—the methods and controls used
to proactively protect an organization from natural or manmade threats
to physical facilities and buildings, as well as physical locations where
information technology is located or work is performed, as in computer
rooms and work locations. Physical and Environmental Security protects
an organization's personnel, electronic equipment, and data/information.

**Procurement**—the application of principles, policies, and procedures
required to plan, apply, and evaluate the purchase of information technology products and services, including risk-based presolicitation, solici-
tation, sources selection award, and monitoring, disposal, and other
post-award activities

**Regulatory and Standards Compliance**—the application of the principles, policies, and procedures that enable an enterprise to meet applicable information security laws, regulations, standards, and policies to
satisfy statutory requirements, perform industry-wide best practices, and
achieve information security program goals

**Security Risk Management**—the policies, processes, procedures, and
technologies used by an organization to create a balanced approach to
identifying and assessing risks to information assets, personnel, facilities,
and equipment, and to manage mitigation strategies that achieve the
security needed at an affordable cost

**Strategic Security Management**—the principles, practices, and methods involved in making managerial decisions and actions that determine the long-term performance of an organization. Strategic security management requires the practice of external business analyses such as customer analyses, competitor analyses, market analyses, and industrial environmental analyses. It also requires the performance of internal business analyses that address financial performance measurement, quality assurance, risk management, and organizational capabilities or constraints. The goal of these analyses is to ensure that an organization's information technology security principles, practices, and system design are in line with its mission statement.

**System and Application Security**—the principles, policies, and procedures pertaining to integrating information security into an information technology system or application during the system development life cycle prior to the operations and maintenance phase. This approach ensures that the operation of information technology systems and software does not present undue risk to the enterprise and its information assets. Supporting activities include risk assessment, risk mitigation, security control selection, implementation and evaluation, and software security standards compliance.

**QUICK FACT**

Cyber security is one of the fastest growing occupational areas in DHS—over 1,000 new positions will be added by 2012.

## THE FUTURE OF CYBER SECURITY

The Department of Homeland Security has assembled an incredible team of experts in the field of information technology. However, many more are needed. DHS announced hiring authority to staff up to 1,000 positions through 2012 across all DHS components to fulfill critical cyber security roles, including analysis, cyber incident response, vulnerability detection and assessment, intelligence and investigation, and network and systems engineering.[2]

The government is committed to equipping DHS with the critical tools necessary to build a world-class cyber organization and compete with the private sector for cyber security talent. Recently, DHS has made inroads in recruiting from the private sector, but they have a long way to go to obtain the future cyberspace leadership that DHS and the federal government has envisioned. The information technology field plays an important function in today's economy and its future functions and security can begin with you.

# CHAPTER seven

## LEGAL CAREERS WITH THE OFFICE OF THE GENERAL COUNSEL

**THE OFFICE** of the General Counsel, comprised of over 1,750 attorneys, is the chief legal counsel for the Department of Homeland Security and is responsible for the entire department's legal determinations. The general counsel is also the DHS regulatory policy officer, managing the rule-making program and ensuring that all regulatory actions comply with relevant statutes and executive orders.

The Office of the General Counsel's central duties include:

▶ providing complete, accurate, and timely legal advice on possible courses of action for DHS

▶ ensuring that DHS policies are implemented lawfully, quickly, and efficiently, to protect the rights and liberties of any Americans who come in contact with DHS

▶ representing DHS in venues throughout the United States, including immigration courts

## AREAS OF PRACTICE

Attorneys of the Office of the General Counsel work at DHS headquarters and throughout all the major components of DHS. Let's examine this further.

### The Office of the General Counsel Headquarters

The Office of the General Counsel is made up of lawyers at DHS headquarters who serve on the general counsel's immediate staff, as well as lawyers working in operating components. The headquarters of the Office of the General Counsel is divided into specialized areas of responsibility, with each division headed by an associate general counsel. The specialized divisions found within the headquarters of the Office of the General Counsel are:

▶ **General Law**
   This division provides legal advice and support on acquisition and procurement activities, labor and employment matters, appropriations and fiscal law issues, general tort and related claims, as well as oversight of the activities of the Board of Correction of Military Records.

▶ **Immigration Law**
   This division provides expertise in United States immigration laws, including deportation and removal, arrest and detention, national security, asylum applications and other remedies, refugee issues, benefit processing and adjudications, inspection and admissibility issues, visa adjudication and issuance, and immigration and federal court litigation.

▶ **Intelligence Law**
   This division provides expertise in authorities related to intelligence collection, analysis, and dissemination; engagement with state, local, tribal, and private sector entities; and information sharing.

▶ **Legal Counsel Law**
   This division provides legal review, guidance, and support on significant litigation matters, including coordinating with the Department

of Justice, and serves as the DHS expert on statutory authorities, including analyzing existing powers and assessing the impact of pending legislation. Legal Counsel also provides legal support on privacy and civil rights and civil liberties issues, and responds to significant inquiries from Congress and the General Accounting Office.

▶ **National Protection and Programs Law**

This division provides legal support to the National Protection and Programs Directorate with specific sections devoted to chemical facility security, communications, cyber security, infrastructure protection, and the US-VISIT program.

▶ **Operations and Enforcement Law**

This division provides expertise in operations, law enforcement, and emergency/incident management activities, including international information exchange, screening and watch lists issues, international agreements and arrangements, foreign investment, and national security reviews.

▶ **Regulatory Affairs Law**

This division leads DHS rule-making activities, coordinates review of proposed regulations, and ensures that all regulatory actions presented to the secretary of the DHS comply with constitutional and statutory restrictions and mandates.

▶ **Technology Programs Law**

This division provides legal support for the Science and Technology Directorate, Domestic Nuclear Detection Office, and Office of Health Affairs.

▶ **Ethics Law**

This division administers the financial disclosure program, coordinates and manages the DHS ethics program that includes providing legal advice, and acts as a liaison to the Office of Government Ethics in the role of Designated Agency Ethics Official, a secretarial appointee.

**QUICK FACT**

The Department of Homeland Security offers students the opportunity to try out positions within the Office of General Counsel through the Honors Program and summer internship programs.

## The Office of the General Counsel Components

The Office of the General Counsel also has attorneys within individual components of the DHS. Each of the Office of the General Counsel components is headed by a chief counsel or its equivalent. These components are found within each of the major offices of the DHS. Here is how those components break down:

▶ **Transportation Security Administration (TSA)**
Responsibilities of the chief counsel and staff of attorneys include providing legal advice to the commissioner and senior leadership of TSA on legal issues associated with their mission. The chief counsel maintains both headquarters and field office locations where TSA missions are conducted. The TSA chief counsel oversees both criminal and civil enforcement of federal laws relating to transportation security, and conducts or manages litigation before courts of administrative tribunals. The chief counsel and lawyers also assist in the development of TSA legislative and regulatory programs, interpreting applicable statutory or regulatory authority, helping shape TSA's legal posture in international matters, and advising TSA on implementing TSA security directives and necessary adjustments to operating procedures.

▶ **Customs and Border Protection (CBP)**
Responsibilities of the CBP chief counsel include providing legal advice to the commissioner and senior CBP leaders on legal issues associated with the CBP mission, as well as providing legal advice and support to all components of CBP, representing CBP in administrative hearings; providing litigation support to the Department of Justice, completing the administrative collection of civil fines and penalties; providing comprehensive legal services to all components of CBP. The CBP chief counsel reviews legislative and regulatory proposals and provides legal training to operational staff. The CBP chief counsel is also responsible for reviewing proposed actions to ensure compliance with legal requirements, preparing formal legal opinions, preparing and reviewing all responses in all civil or criminal court actions involving CBP; and developing nationwide programs,

policies, and procedures within its functional area. The CBP chief counsel has both a headquarters office and field structure. The headquarters is divided broadly into three functional areas: ethics, labor and employment; enforcement; and trade and finance. Each of these functional areas is under the supervision of associate chief counsels. The field structure consists of associate and assistant chief counsels, located in major cities across the United States, who advise field managers in their geographical areas.

▶ **United States Citizenship and Immigration Service (USCIS)**
Responsibilities of the USCIS chief counsel include providing legal advice to the director and senior leadership of USCIS on legal issues associated with USCIS missions, as well as providing legal support to USCIS components and the Department of Justice office in the area of immigration litigation; providing legal advice on the adjudication of applicants for temporary visa status, permanent residence, citizenship, and asylum. The USCIS chief counsel also offers legal education and training to USCIS personnel; reviews legislative and regulatory proposals; and represents USCIS in visa petitions appeals and in administrative proceedings. The USCIS chief counsel maintains a headquarters location as well as field offices supporting the USCIS components throughout the United States.

▶ **Immigration and Customs Enforcement (ICE)**
ICE principle legal advisors oversee the largest legal component in DHS with more than 900 attorneys from the Office of the General Counsel. The principle legal advisors provide legal advice to the assistant secretary and other senior ICE leaders on legal issues associated with the ICE mission. The ICE principle legal advisors also represent ICE in all exclusion, deportation, and removal proceedings; prosecuting removal court cases and handling Board of Immigration Appeal cases. The ICE advisors also provide litigation support to United States Attorney offices, assisting with removal order reinstatements, administrative removal orders, and expedited removals. Legal advisors also review legislative and regulatory proposals and provide training and ethics guidance to all ICE personnel. Legal advisors represent ICE in court and other administrative proceedings.

▶ **United States Secret Service (USSS)**

Responsibilities of the Secret Service chief counsel include providing legal advice to the director and other senior Secret Service leaders on legal issues associated with the Secret Service protective and investigative missions, and its administrative responsibilities. The Secret Service chief counsel provides support to the Department of Justice in their claims against the Secret Service and its employees. The Secret Service chief counsel prepares comments on proposed legislative and regulatory proposals; drafts testimony and policy; directs the Secret Service ethics program; and reviews documents related to assets forfeiture. The Secret Service chief counsel also makes determinations concerning release of information under the Freedom of Information Act, criminal and civil discovery, subpoenas and other requests, as well as represents the Secret Service in administrative hearings.

▶ **Federal Emergency Management Agency (FEMA)**

Responsibilities of FEMA chief counsel include providing legal advice to the administrator and senior leadership of FEMA on legal issues associated with FEMA missions as well as interpreting applicable statutory and regulatory authority with respect to disaster and emergency assistance, national preparedness, National Continuity Programs, the National Flood Insurance Program, and the National Response Framework. FEMA chief counsel conducts or manages litigation before courts and administrative tribunals; provides legal advice on fiscal law issues, procurement actions, and the Freedom of Information and Privacy Act. FEMA chief counsel also reviews legislative and regulatory proposals, and provides training and counseling through the Alternative Dispute Resolution Program to reduce complaints against FEMA and improve workplace communication and coordination.

▶ **United States Coast Guard (USCG)**

Responsibilities of the USCG judge advocate general include providing legal advice to the commandant and other senior USCG leadership in areas including international and maritime law, including drug and alien interdiction; counterterrorism; defense operations, marine safety and facilitating maritime commerce, and protecting living marine resources and the environment. The USCG judge advocate general, with a staff of over 280 attorneys, develops legal services throughout the Coast Guard to support mission execution; manages the Coast Guard Legal Program, military justice, litigation and claims; and handles legislation and rule-making, environmental law, legal assistance, and major systems acquisitions.

▶ **Federal Law Enforcement Training Center (FLETC)**
Responsibilities of the FLETC chief counsel include providing legal advice to the director and senior leadership of FLETC on legal issues associated with FLETC missions, as well as representing FLETC equal opportunity and employment disciplinary cases, and representing FLETC in administrative hearings. The FLETC chief counsel provides legal advice and assistance in procurement-related matters. The Federal Law Enforcement Training Center chief counsel represents FLETC in bid protest and contract disputes, processing and adjudicating claims under the Military and Civilian Employees Compensation Act and Federal Tort Claims Act. Federal Law Enforcement Training Center chief counsel also provides legal advice and assistance on fiscal law issues and legislative matters, information/intellectual law matters to include copyright, the Freedom of Information Act, and the Privacy Act. As well, the chief counsel provides legal training for federal, state, local, and international law enforcement officers attending basic and advanced training at the Federal Law Enforcement Training Center's four domestic and two international training sites.

## OPPORTUNITIES TO PRACTICE LAW

If you are an accomplished lawyer or currently studying law, the Office of General Counsel with DHS may be a place to consider. You will have the opportunity to practice law in an environment that shapes the future of the government of the United States while protecting its citizens from terrorist threats.

The Office of the General Counsel has several programs in place to assist entry-level hiring of up-and-coming legal students.

## Honors Program

The Honors Program serves as a cornerstone for entry-level attorney hiring by the DHS. It offers highly qualified third-year law students, graduates, and judicial law clerks the opportunity to start their legal career with the Office of the General Counsel. Honor Program attorneys are hired for a two-year term, during which they have the opportunity to work in the headquarters of the Office of the General Counsel and other participating component legal offices within the Office of the General Counsel.

The responsibilities offered the Honors Program attorneys include litigation, administrative law, commercial law, procurement law, legislative and regulatory drafting, maritime law, immigration law, and national security law. The participants are given a significant amount of responsibility early on in their careers and can expect to handle highly visible and legally significant cases on an accelerated basis. All participants who achieve satisfactory performance ratings during their two-year term become eligible for full-time positions, depending on the needs of the department and available funding. The selection process is highly competitive. Candidates are selected on the basis of: academic achievement, writing ability, law review or moot court experience, legal aid or clinical experience, and work history.

## Summer Law Intern Program

The Summer Law Intern Program is designed to introduce law interns to the operating components of the Office of the General Counsel within the DHS. Successful candidates will be given the opportunity to work in the different legal divisions of the Office of the General Counsel including: immigration, regulatory affairs, operations and enforcement, legal counsel, general law, technology programs, national protection programs, and intelligence. The Department of Homeland Security selects the interns based on: academic achievement, writing ability, law review or moot court experi-ence, legal aid, or clinical experience, and work history.

## Volunteer Legal Intern/Extern Program

The Volunteer Legal Intern/Extern Program uses on the same application criteria as the Summer Law Intern Program but accepts interns and externs on a volunteer basis. Interns in this program are able to gather the same le-gal experiences of the Office of the General Counsel, but as volunteers they do not receive compensation.

Besides these programs, the Office of the General Counsel regularly posts vacancy announcements at the headquarters level and throughout the United States. We show you how to find job announcements in Chapter 9, as well as how to network with employees within the Office of the General Counsel in Chapter 13. The rewards and job satisfaction found working at the highest levels of government for the Office of the General Counsel can be immense; if you are a working or aspiring attorney who wants to really make a difference, it may be the place for you.

# CHAPTER eight

## CAREERS IN ACQUISITIONS

**THE DEPARTMENT** of Homeland Security acquisitions program is the third-largest procurement budget in the federal government at more than $20 billion annually. In addition, according to a report from the Office of the Inspector General, the American Recovery and Reinvestment Act of 2009 has provided the DHS with approximately $2.8 billion to acquire goods and services to help stimulate the United States economy. According to this report, the DHS does not have enough trained and qualified staff to fulfill the responsibilities of contracting officers, contracting officer technical representatives, program project managers, and grant managers. It goes on to say that competition with other departments in the federal government for acquisition personnel is intense, and may become more intense with the additional requirements of the American Recovery and Reinvestment Act of 2009 at multiple agencies. The existing shortage of skilled, federal acquisition personnel adversely affects the capacity of the DHS to manage mission critical programs and represents a risk to the Recovery Act investments.[1]

The Department of Homeland Security is actively engaged in recruiting professionals with contracting experience to manage their operational acquisitions of supplies and services. In this chapter we discuss the options available to you in the area of acquisitions or government contracting.

**QUICK FACT**

The Department of Homeland Security purchases over $20 billion worth of assets every year.

## WHAT IS ACQUISITIONS?

Let's start out with a definition of acquisitions:

> *"Acquisition" means the acquiring by contract with appropriated funds of supplies or services (including construction) by and for the use of federal government through purchase or lease, whether the supplies or services are already in existence or must be created, developed, demonstrated, and evaluated. Acquisition begins at the point when agency needs are established and includes the description of the requirement to satisfy agency needs, solicitation and selection of sources, award of contract, contract financing, contract performance, contract administration, and those technical and management functions directly related to the process of fulfilling agency need by contract.*[2]

Acquisition or contracting responsibilities include the following: preparing initial drafts of requests for proposals, contracts, and support documentation; assisting the contract managers and program managers in developing requirements and acquisition plans and strategies; drafting contracts, purchase orders, delivery orders, and contract modifications for contract managers to review. The acquisitions career field is also responsible for administering contracts including processing invoices, monitoring contract provisions, and ensuring contractor performance; preparing documentation for the contract file; and compiling and analyzing contract data. Contract managers have signature authority for authorized contractual business and act as negotiators, coordinating with agency and legal counsel, audit, and program offices.

The Department of Homeland Security is looking for acquisition or contract specialists with education in business management, engineering, law, accounting, or related fields, and with experience in government contracting, administration, commercial purchasing, or their related fields. It is also looking for acquisition specialists with knowledge of acquisition policies, and procedures, and other applicable regulations. Contract specialists and managers in acquisitions are utilized within major components of the DHS, including the Coast Guard, Customs and Border Protection, the Transportation Security Administration, Immigration and Customs Enforcement, the Secret Service, the Federal Emergency Management Agency, and the Federal Law Enforcement Training Center.

## ENTRANCE TO ACQUISITIONS CAREERS

The Department of Homeland Security has several programs available to encourage hiring in the area of acquisitions. The following details these acquisition career path programs:

## ACQUISITION PROFESSIONAL CAREER PROGRAM

Applicants chosen for this program are appointed to three, one-year rotational assignments in different DHS component organizations, providing them with the opportunity to gain experience in a wide variety of work environments. In Acquisition Professional Career Programs (APCPs) you may work in short-notice disaster relief planning efforts at FEMA, long-term ship design projects at the Coast Guard, ongoing screening and detection equipment development testing and deployment for the TSA, or other vital projects and programs throughout the DHS. The experience gained, combined with the training and mentorship program that is discussed later, will enhance your understanding and comprehension of an acquisition career field, preparing you for virtually any situation you may encounter during your career. The APCP additionally provides a broader perspective into the many missions going on simultaneously within the DHS. This allows you to see both the parts and the whole picture that work toward the larger DHS mission protecting against and

responding to threats and hazards facing the United States. APCP participants will be required to choose the business track or the technical track.

In the **Business Track**, participants become 1102 series contract specialists, developing requirements and determining the best value among proposals. After determining the best value, the contract specialists will sign the
contracts on behalf of the federal government.

In the **Technical Track**, participants train in one of several available occupational series:

▶ program manager (242 series)
▶ systems engineering (801 series)
▶ industrial engineering (896 series)
▶ information technology specialist (2210 series)

Each of these series manages the design, development, and deployment of
new technologies vital to the protection of the United States.

(Note: These series job descriptions have been previously discussed in
Chapter 2.)

New hire prospects are started at a GS-07 series grade level, appointed
for a three-year rotational period to learn the various operational missions
in the DHS. Upon successful completion of the program, a hire will be
placed into a permanent full-time position, with promotion up to a GS-13
series grade level.

## TRAINING

The Acquisition Professional Career Program provides the skills and training necessary to become a sought-after expert in the field of acquisition.
Through the program, the DHS invests over 400 hours of technical training. As you progress through the program you will receive progressively
higher certifications within your acquisitions career field. These certifications are recognized throughout the federal government and will serve as
your professional credentials as a recognized expert in your field. Additionally, you will receive more than 100 hours of leadership-specific training.

This leadership training will provide you with the skills to become a future leader in tomorrow's government.

## MENTORING

Within the first 90 days of the program you will be partnered with a senior expert in your acquisition field who will provide you with positive guidance on how to reach your full potential. Along with the experienced professionals you will have the opportunity to work with and learn from on a daily basis, you will be able to turn to your mentor for frank discussion, advice, and career planning. Together, you will assess your professional strengths and weaknesses to develop a mentoree action plan, laying out your long-term career goals and aspirations. Your mentor will work with you over the length of your participation in the APCP, helping you on the road to your professional success.

The APCP hiring process is a lengthy one. The application can take several months to process. Applicants are encouraged to apply at the earliest date possible. The APCP applicants are required to be United States citizens; they must be able to obtain a security clearance, as required by all DHS procurement jobs. (The security clearance process is discussed in Chapter 12.)

In an effort to develop a talented and diverse group of procurement specialists, DHS is utilizing active recruiters to find the kind of contracting professionals they desire. Acquisition Professional Career Program representatives will be attending recruiting events across the United States. The Department of Homeland Security is participating in numerous college recruitment events, national conferences, and career fairs. The Department of Homeland Security has also partnered with minority servicing institutions and veterans' organizations to reach minority and military communities, as well as people with disabilities.[3] The recruiting events are the perfect opportunity to seek further information on the Acquisition Professional Career

Program and your opportunities within the federal government as an Acquisition Specialist.

## CONTRACT SPECIALISTS POSITIONS FOR ANNUITANTS

Office of Personal Management projections indicate that disproportionate numbers of current federal workers will become retirement-eligible through 2010, with the highest number of these being contract specialists.[4] The Department of Homeland Security is seeking to reemploy federal annuitants with contracting experience. If you have retired from federal service as a Business Track GS-1102 series in the grade range of GS-13 to GS-15, you may qualify to join the Homeland Security procurement team without sacrificing your existing retirement annuity. You will have the opportunity to serve in limited-term appointments. You may also have the opportunity to serve as a mentor to participants of the Acquisition Professional Career Program.

## LATERAL TRANSFERS

If you are a current federal employee employed outside the Department of Homeland Security and are currently engaged in federal contracting activities, the DHS is actively seeking you as well. Current federal employees have the opportunity to apply directly with the DHS, bypassing the federal vacancy announcements, and sending their resumes via e-mail to: acquisition professionals@dhs.gov. Due to the shortages previously discussed in this chapter, your experience in federal contracting is greatly needed.

With DHS having the third-largest procurement budget in the federal government and the continued importance of DHS missions in the protection of the United States, acquisition career professionals will continue to be in increasing demand. If you are a specialist in the field of federal contracting, you need to look seriously at the opportunities available with a career in acquisitions.

# CHAPTER nine

## WHAT ARE THE OPPORTUNITIES?

**THE DEPARTMENT** of Homeland Security offers more opportunities to match your job skills and interests than any other federal government department or agency. But with so many choices, it's a daunting task to sort through the variety of career titles to locate jobs that interest you and for which you are qualified. This chapter helps you sift through the opportunities and target the DHS career that's a fit for you.

## WHERE ARE THE OPPORTUNITIES?

The Department of Homeland Security is developing into an organization that is leading the United States in a new area of security and innovation, and its role in today's world is ever evolving. With the constantly changing economic climate, new challenges are added to the DHS's missions and it has initiated steps to meet those challenges by establishing career positions that not only protect, but analyze, predict, and plan for future happenings. The

DHS is on the cutting edge of technology, planning and developing the future innovations that will be utilized by federal, state, and local government agencies.

## QUICK FACT

The Department of Homeland Security expects to fill 65,730 mission-critical jobs by 2012.

Having a team in place that can meet the security challenges for the future is critical to the stability of the United States, and to meet those challenges the DHS expects to fill 65,730 mission-critical jobs by 2012, and that number doesn't include the additional non-mission-critical jobs that need to be filled on a regular basis. The table breaks down, by occupational area, of the expected DHS mission-critical hires for 2010–2012.

## Department of Homeland Security 2010–2012 Hiring Projections

| Occupational Area | Projected Hires 2010–2012 |
| --- | --- |
| Accounting and budget analysis | 220 |
| Adjudication officers | 2,250 |
| Asylum officers | 155 |
| Attorneys | 745 |
| Border patrol agents | 9,800 |
| Contract representatives | 90 |
| Contracting | 875 |
| Criminal investigation | 1,410 |
| Customs and border protection | 4,950 |
| Engineering | 375 |
| General biological sciences (agricultural sciences) | 970 |
| General investigation, investigation and compliance | 3,000 |
| Human resources | 430 |
| Immigration enforcement | 1,150 |

| | |
|---|---|
| Import specialists | 125 |
| Information technology | 1,025 |
| Intelligence analysis | 390 |
| Management/program analysis | 1,850 |
| Physical sciences | 125 |
| Police officers | 470 |
| Security administration | 825 |
| Transportation security officers | 34,500 |
| **Total:** | **65,730** |

*Source:* Department of Homeland Security, "Where the Jobs Are 2009, Mission Critical Opportunities for America," http://data.wherethejobsare.org/wtja/agency/31, Sept 23, 2009.

The Department of Homeland Security's workforce is influenced by a number of factors, including technological advances, expanded mission responsibilities, and a continuing terror threat. Couple this with the projected retirement of employees annually in the entire federal government reaching a high of 61.3% by the year 2016,[1] and one begins to see the career opportunities available within the DHS.

The hiring projections through 2012[2] indicate that the top five job categories in the federal government will be in:

1. Medical and public health
2. Security and protection
3. Compliance and enforcement
4. Legal
5. Administrative and program management

## WHAT IS IN DHS'S FUTURE?

Homeland security is a new core component of our government. In the establishment of the DHS, government leaders set goals and parameters not only in operational priorities, but in personnel and future governmental leadership. This innovative policy agenda has set the DHS apart from other agencies and departments and has established new career opportunities for you and your future.

**QUICK FACT**

The 2010 budget for the DHS was $42.7 billion.

The budget of the DHS has increased annually since 2001. With each funding increase has come an increase in personnel to handle the workload. The agency's 2010 budget was $42.7 billion,[3] and keeping with the trend, will be even larger in the years to come.

There are countless career opportunities available because of the broad nature of the DHS mission. As you have been reading this book and learning what each department and agency within DHS does, we hope that you have also been thinking about how the various careers relate to your interests and skills. Undoubtedly, with the vast array of DHS careers available, at least one career touched on in this book will pique your interest. Once you have determined your area of interest and read everything we have provided on that career choice, be sure to refer to the Appendixes at the back of the book for more source material that will help you learn more about your specific career interest.

## WHERE TO LOCATE JOB OPENINGS

It's important to understand how the federal government determines eligibilities for a specific position within the federal government. There are two classes of jobs found in federal government—competitive and excepted service.

**Competitive Service** jobs fall under the jurisdiction of the Office of Personnel Management. These jobs are subject to laws passed by Congress that ensure that applicants and employees receive fair and equal treatment in the hiring process. They give selecting officials broad authority to review more than one applicant source before determining the best qualified candidate based on job-related criteria. A basic principle is that all candidates must meet the qualifications for the position to which they are appointed.

In filling competitive service jobs, agencies generally choose from three groups of candidates.

1. **A competitive list of eligible applicants.** This record lists the applicants, in rank order, who meet the qualification requirements for a specific vacancy announcement.

2. **A list of eligible applicants who have civil service status.** This list consists of applicants who are eligible for noncompetitive movement within the competitive service. These individuals presently or previously served in career-type appointments in the competitive service. They are selected under agency merit promotion procedures and can receive an appointment by promotion, reassignment, transfer, or reinstatement.

3. **A list of eligible applicants who qualify for a special noncompetitive appointing authority established by law or executive order.** An example of special noncompetitive appointing authority would include: Veteran's Readjustment Appointment, the special authority for 30% or more disabled veterans, or the Peace Corps.

**Excepted Service** jobs are found in federal agencies that set their own qualification requirements. These agencies are not subject to the appointment, pay, and classification rules of laws established by Congress. They are, however, subject to veteran's preference rules. Some federal agencies (such as the FBI and CIA) only have Excepted Service positions. Other agencies may have some divisions or even specific jobs that may be excepted from civil service procedures. Excepted Service allows the agency to fill positions in unusual or special hiring needs. These positions may be excepted by law, executive order, or by action of the Office of Personnel Management.

Agencies in the competitive service are required by law and the Office of Personnel Management to post vacancies with the Office of Personnel Management whenever they are seeking candidates from outside their own workforce for positions lasting more than 120 days. These vacancies are posted on the Office of Personnel Management's USAJOBS and STUDENTJOBS sites. Excepted agencies are not required to post their job announcements with the Office of Personnel Management. To learn about their job opportunities in excepted service positions one must go to the specific agency's website.

## UNDERSTANDING JOB CLASSIFICATIONS

The Office of Personnel Management has established job occupational groups and series used to classify the work positions. The classification is made in terms of the kind or subject matter of work, the level of difficulty and responsibility, and the qualification requirements of the job. You need to understand what the listing means when you are searching for careers within the DHS; this will assist you in determining matches with your interests, training, and abilities. To better help you get a grasp on these classifications, the Office of Personnel Management has published a comprehensive "Introduction to the Position Classification Standards" document, which is free to download here:

www.opm.gov/fedclass/GSintro.pdf

## WHERE TO FIND THE JOB ANNOUNCEMENTS

In an effort to streamline federal job announcements, the federal government has established **USAJOBS.GOV**, a website dedicated to posting *most* of the job openings found throughout the government. However, the word *most* is key here—the listings are not all-inclusive and some agencies and departments do not utilize it for specific jobs/classifications, especially for excepted agencies. If you are serious about getting a career in the DHS, it is in your best interest to check both USAJOBS.GOV and the individual websites for each agency or department.

These federal websites offer you the flexibility to search on your terms. They are easily accessible, and are available 24 hours a day, seven days a week; best of all, they are free of charge to use. Be leery of other websites that offer for a fee to do what you can for free on an official government website.

## About USAJOBS.GOV and STUDENTJOBS.GOV

**www.usajobs.gov** is operated by the Office of Personnel Management and is the federal government's official portal for federal jobs and employment information. The website is described as your "one-stop source for Federal jobs and employment information" and is continually updated to provide the most comprehensive listing of federal job opportunities available. USAJOBS also provides you with training tutorials and guides on effectively utilizing the website to make your job searching more effective.

**www.studentjobs.gov** is also operated by the Office of Personnel Management and is the official portal for students looking for federal jobs and employment information. This website provides students with the essential knowledge they need to search for and embark on a new federal career. The website also offers students information on finding a specific interest in federal government employment by exploring summer internships, fellowships, grants, and loan repayment programs.

## SEARCHING FOR A JOB WITH USAJOBS.GOV

At any one time, tens of thousands of federal career opportunities can be found on USAJOBS.GOV. Utilizing the search function, you can narrow your searches to jobs within the DHS, jobs within a specific job classification, title, location, salary or pay grade, or category listing interests.

## Getting Started

Start by logging on to www.usajobs.gov. On the homepage, you will be given the opportunity to research your interests and view the latest trends, learn the federal hiring process, search for jobs listed, create an account where you can save your searches, create automated job alerts, upload your resume, and apply for position vacancies. Using this website to land the federal job you want is a three-step process.

### Step 1

If you are serious about a career with the federal government we suggest that you create a free account. Your information is protected and backed by federal law. With an account you can save your searches, save the jobs that interest you, and have the ability to create and store your federal resume for use when you apply for your future career with the DHS. The website will walk you through creating an account.

### Step 2

When you are ready to begin your search for a job with the DHS, simply utilize the "Search Jobs" function found on the homepage. Here you can enter keywords (such as *investigator*, *engineer*, *attorney*, etc.) to begin your search. Try to be as specific as possible. If you type in a broad search term such as *Department of Homeland Security*, you get a good idea of just how many opportunities are to be found in the agency, but you'll quickly see the need to narrow your search to cover your interests and skill level.

Once you find an interesting job opportunity, click on the specific announcement to see an overview that contains all the basic information about the job, such as the salary, open period, and who may apply, as well as a brief summary of the agency, job, and key requirements. Important items to note on this page are the opening and closing dates of the announcement.

Most online federal job announcements contain Overview, Duties, Qualifications & Evaluations, Benefits & Other Info, and How to Apply categories. Take the time to explore each of these areas. You'll learn about the major job duties and get a detailed overview of the day-to-day job responsibilities, as well as the qualifications and experience needed to apply. You'll learn how you will be evaluated for the position and learn what federal benefits the job has to offer, as well as any other pertinent information the agency wants you to know. In the How to Apply area, you will find directions on how to apply for that specific job, including agency contact information and what to expect after you apply for the position. Pay close attention to the information found here; you do not want to find out that your application was rejected because you did not follow the instructions as to the requirements of the announcement.

In reading the job announcement, consider how this job relates to your interests, experience, and training. You will quickly be able to determine if this announcement is one that you wish to pursue. If it is, be sure to save the link; you will need to refer to it again and again while you create your federal resume, which is discussed in Chapter 11.

## Step 3

In this final step you should utilize all the resources available on USAJOBS.GOV to gather all the information and advice so you can be successful in your searches and application process. The website offers you the opportunity to explore your interests and assists you in narrowing your interests. You'll find links to tutorials and guides to help you understand everything from searching techniques to creating a portfolio. You can research the hot federal careers, look at trends in federal hiring, learn the federal hiring process, and discover secrets to getting your application noticed.

The process of locating a job and applying for a position within the DHS may seem daunting. When you utilize USAJOBS.GOV and STUDENTJOBS.GOV properly, they can go a long way toward taking the fear out of the process.

Devote time to your job searches, and research all the tutorials and guides available. You are making a decision of a lifetime. Spending time to understand each step will make the process of applying for a federal position much easier and, ultimately, successful.

# CHAPTER ten

## FINDING YOUR CAREER FIT

**THE OFFICE** of Personnel Management publishes qualification standards for each job within the DHS to help ensure that employees can successfully and safely perform the work required for that position. Your skills and training may qualify you to meet the minimum standards for many different jobs. However, when applying for a position within the federal government, keep in mind that the DHS is looking for the most highly qualified personnel to fill the positions. There may be a thousand or more applicants for one or two highly desired positions. The position description states the minimum required education for the position. You must have skills, knowledge, experience, and education that will set you apart from the other applicants.

## QUICK FACT

The Department of Homeland Security can receive over 1,000 job applications for one or two openings in highly sought after career fields.

## QUALIFICATIONS

The Department of Homeland Security hires personnel with all levels of education and experience. Employees range from students fresh out of high school with little or no experience, to highly trained and educated personnel with doctoral degrees and established careers. Each job announcement indicates the qualifications for the position and the evaluations utilized to select the best qualified candidate. The following table contains a breakdown of the government's General Schedule and related requirements to meet each level.

| GRADE | QUALIFYING EDUCATION |
| --- | --- |
| GS-1 | None |
| GS-2 | High school graduation or equivalent |
| GS-3 | 1 academic year above high school |
| GS-4 | 2 academic years above high school, **or** associate's degree |
| GS-5 | 4 academic years above high school leading to a bachelor's degree, **or** bachelor's degree |
| GS-7 | Bachelor's degree with superior academic achievement for two-grade interval positions, **or** 1 academic year of graduate education (or law school, as specified in qualification standards or individual occupational requirements) |
| GS-9 | Master's (or equivalent graduate degree such as LLB or JD as specified in qualification standards or individual occupational requirements), **or** 2 academic years of progressively higher level graduate education |
| GS-11 | PhD or equivalent doctoral degree, **or** 3 academic years of progressively higher level graduate education, **or** *For research positions only*, completion of all requirements for a master's or equivalent degree |
| GS-12 | *For research positions only*, completion of all requirements for a doctoral or equivalent degree |

*Source:* http://www.opm.gov/qualifications/policy/ApplicationOfStds-04.asp.

## EXPERIENCE VERSUS EDUCATION

At the lower GS levels, college education may not be necessary. Your specialized experience may be acceptable in lieu of a formal degree. Starting at the GS-5 level, positions generally require one year of specialized experience equal to the next lower grade level. Your life experiences count in the federal government in qualifying you for the job position. The Department of Homeland Security will evaluate your experience as it relates to the position qualifications and rank your work experiences, accomplishments, education, training, and overall background against the qualification requirements for the position.

## SECONDARY EDUCATION LEVEL CAREERS

Due to the nature of the missions of the DHS, increasingly specialized skills and education requirements are required for many positions. Jobs in some occupations such as engineers, lawyers, contracting, and physical sciences will require an advanced major field of study or completion of specific academic programs at the graduate level (such as JD, PhD, DBA, PsyD, MD). These positions generally start at the GS-9 to GS-12 level.

There are many occupations where a baccalaureate degree in any field of study is acceptable. Some requirements may call for a general baccalaureate degree and specific work experience while others may call for specific degrees but will accept little or no work experience. These positions generally start at the GS-7 to GS-9 levels. With some positions, job-related experience can be as good as a formal education. Your work experience may meet the requirements to increase your level on the GS scale. Your level of experience and/or specific baccalaureate degree should not deter you from pursuing a new career with the DHS.

## EDUCATION IN HOMELAND SECURITY

Since September 11, 2001, significant advances have been made to increase the level of competence in the Department of Homeland Security. The federal government has acknowledged that it needs to commit to long-term training and education programs that will provide the expertise needed in the field of homeland security. Thus, it has begun to initiate training and certification programs to make the department more effective in the future to respond to its critical missions.

Following September 11th and the creation of the DHS, educational institutions around the world saw a need to create a new degree program tailored specifically to homeland security careers. Now, several institutions are offering bachelor's, master's, and doctoral degrees with a concentration in homeland security. These new degrees are a hybrid combination of political science, military strategy, criminal justice, and emergency management.

Potential homeland security students should be cautioned that many programs have advertised themselves as "homeland security degrees," but offer very little actual knowledge in homeland security. Many of these programs offer nothing more than business degrees or political science degrees with a couple of classes added that discuss "hot topics" in homeland security. These programs are usually classified as business degree with a concentration in homeland security, rather than a specific homeland security degree.

To date, several institutions offer bachelor's and master's degrees in homeland security. However, only a handful of schools offer doctoral degrees in homeland security. Many of these programs are available online or in the typical classroom format.

### QUICK FACT

The Naval Postgraduate School's Center for Homeland Defense and Security is the only program that is officially endorsed by the Department of Homeland Security. Tuition for this program is free, but admission is highly selective and limited only to people who have executive roles in homeland security.

The Naval Postgraduate School's Center for Homeland Defense and Security (CHDS) in Monterey, California, is the only program that is officially endorsed by the Department of Homeland Security. It's a cooperative program between the Department of Defense, the Department of Homeland Security, and the Federal Emergency Management Agency. CHDS was started in 2002 after there was found to be a need for a program that would develop leadership centered around the war on terrorism.

The mission of the CHDS program is "To strengthen the national security of the United States by providing graduate level educational programs and services that meet the immediate and long-term leadership needs of organizations responsible for homeland defense and security."[1] It has two specific program goals:

▶ strengthen national capacity for homeland security by advancing the study of homeland security as a substantive field of research, scholarship, and professional discipline
▶ create a "multiplier effect" to maximize federal investment—share program content, research results, and educational resources with organizations across the nation to build national homeland security preparedness through education

The CHDS offers two separate tracks. The first is the on-campus, postgraduate degree program, and the other program is the noncredit track that allows an eligible candidate to attend online courses. The CHDS offers several degrees, including a Master of Arts in National Security Affairs and a Master of Business Administration with a Defense Focus. The selection process for this free program is very competitive, and is reserved for people who are in executive positions in various local, state, and federal government agencies. Applicants must also commit to working in a homeland security role for at least five years following completion of the degree program.

Personnel who are not eligible for the degree program can still take noncredit courses that are offered online. To be eligible to take these courses, applicants must demonstrate that they are in a position that requires them to have the knowledge offered in the courses. The noncredit courses are security-sensitive, and an application must be completed prior to approval. These courses include:

- ▶ Research Process and Methods
- ▶ Technology for Homeland Security: Inspection and Detection Technologies
- ▶ Critical Infrastructure: Vulnerability Analysis and Protection
- ▶ The Global Jihadi Threat
- ▶ Homeland Security in Israel

To obtain more information about the courses offered at the Naval Postgraduate School Center for Defense and Homeland Security visit www.cdhs.us.

## CERTIFICATIONS IN HOMELAND SECURITY

Secondary educational institutions in the United States have added certificate programs, associate's, bachelor's, and master's degree programs specializing in homeland security. Since 2001, over 300 colleges and universities in the United States have created degree programs in homeland security.[2] Education programs have also developed in the homeland security technical trades and analytical aspects of the careers found in the DHS. For the future or current student who is thinking of pursuing a career with the DHS, there is a new and emerging area of educational study—a degree in homeland security. These new education opportunities offer a challenging option. Numerous accredited colleges and universities have been working with the DHS to establish curriculum to provide the necessary education to train professionals with the skills needed to lead the United States. The study in homeland security will give individuals a broad overview of the operations of the DHS, and prepare them for the specialties needed for the future.

A degree in homeland security is appropriate for applicants who will be applying for positions that have a broad range of homeland security responsibilities such as managerial positions, criminal investigators, or intelligence analysts. Some positions accept a wide range of degrees in the area of specialty, while other positions may require a very specific degree. The position that you desire within the DHS will determine the most appropriate degree for that position and if you are uncertain as to what degree would be most appropriate for your desired position, study the job description or call a DHS recruiter.

**QUICK FACT**

When choosing a college or university to attend, make sure that the school is accredited. Schools that are not accredited are not recognized by the DHS.

Secondary education in homeland security should include a combination of theory and practical application courses. The courses should include a variety of disciplines, such as criminal justice, law, emergency management, counterterrorism, intelligence, social science, security management, and communications. Curriculum should also address the interagency skills specifically designed to fulfill the responsibilities of DHS. The courses that you attend should match your career goals. Educators should possess real-world experience to provide you with the education and necessary skills to complete the missions of the DHS.

The following is a list of specialized subjects that you could expect to cover if you were pursuing a degree in homeland security:

► emergency planning
► introduction to terrorism
► aviation security
► maritime security
► cargo and shipping security
► cyber security
► cyber law
► computer crimes
► information warfare
► public policy
► criminal intelligence
► foreign intelligence
► counterintelligence
► psychology of terrorism
► economics of terrorism and disaster

▶ weapons of mass destruction

▶ border and coastal security

▶ disaster preparedness and recovery

▶ security system evaluation

▶ risk analysis

▶ chemical and biological risk defense

▶ religion and terrorism

▶ Islamic fundamentalism

## CHOOSING A SCHOOL

The Department of Homeland Security will not recognize degrees from schools that lack accreditation. To date, the majority of accredited schools that offer a specific homeland security degree do so using online training. This allows the student to attend classes via the Internet, without having to physically attend classes. Despite the lack of a formal classroom environment, the course work is just as rigorous and demanding as one would find at a traditional school. Attending class online allows for greater flexibility for the student. Many programs are set up to allow the students to work at their own pace, going as fast or as slow as they want to through the program. However, one of the greatest drawbacks to an online program is the lack of networking that occurs with a traditional campus. Many online schools are addressing this by requiring students to attend week-long functions annually on campus to bring the students together.

As with any undergraduate degree program, be prepared to spend your first two years completing your general education requirements such as math, English, foreign language, and life sciences. Most students in a bachelor's degree program do not begin taking their degree-specific classes until their junior and senior year.

Another important consideration when choosing a school is to look at the experience of the faculty. Ask to see the biographies of the instructors who will be teaching your classes. Your instructors and professors should be well-versed in homeland security. They should have experience working in actual homeland security positions, and should have graduate-level or doctoral degrees. A lot of college programs will assign the students a mentor to follow their progress throughout their college education. Students may be allowed to choose from a list mentors who best match their needs. Assigning a mentor to students can prove to be an invaluable resource as the students complete their college degree.

Some experts argue that a degree in homeland security may not be the best degree to obtain. They argue that the degree is too generic, and does not give the student enough knowledge to be effective in any specific area of homeland security. These experts argue that potential students should pursue a specific degree in an area of expertise that is needed by the Department of Homeland Security. These areas would include foreign language, government policy, accounting, computer science, and so forth. By obtaining a degree in a specific area of expertise, you will increase your chance of success in obtaining a particular position. However, a specific degree can also work to limit the number of positions to which you are eligible to apply. If you have any questions regarding the most appropriate degree, review the position descriptions, or contact a DHS recruiter.

Following is just an example of the types of degrees one could obtain that would be beneficial for a career in homeland security:

- ▶ Criminal justice
- ▶ Fire protection
- ▶ Middle Eastern studies
- ▶ Disaster preparedness
- ▶ Emergency management
- ▶ Accounting
- ▶ Political science
- ▶ Computer science
- ▶ Life sciences (biology, chemistry, psychology, sociology)
- ▶ Financial security
- ▶ Counterterrorism
- ▶ Criminal intelligence/counterintelligence
- ▶ Military science
- ▶ Biosecurity
- ▶ Foreign language studies

▶ Foreign policy
▶ Criminology
▶ Law
▶ Medicine

## PAYING FOR SCHOOL

Consider scholarship, fellowships, and internships with the DHS to assist you in paying for your college. Utilizing these basic steps will help you when it comes to landing that future career in the DHS. The Department of Homeland Security has budgeted $50 million a year for grants and scholarships. Most of these grants and scholarships are available through the college or university that is offering the degree. A lot of the money for this program goes toward reducing the cost of tuition for students who enroll in courses that would be beneficial to the DHS. In 2005, the following colleges and universities received over $30 million from the DHS to develop new programs of study in the field of homeland security.[3]

▶ University of Maryland, Baltimore
▶ University of Tennessee, Knoxville
▶ Eastern Michigan University
▶ Michigan State University
▶ Homeland Security Institute
▶ Florida State University
▶ George Washington University
▶ American College of Emergency Physicians
▶ Dartmouth College

For those students who cannot afford to attend college, an excellent option is to join the military. The military offers exceptional educational benefits, including repayment of student loans, and the G.I. Bill. The military also has deals worked out with several colleges and universities throughout the world to offer steeply discounted tuition rates to active and former military personnel. For more information on the educational incentives offered with the Department of Defense, contact a military recruiter near you or visit http://www.gibill.va.gov/.

---

**QUICK FACT**

The Department of Homeland Security has budgeted $50 million a year for grants and scholarships for those students who are pursuing an education in homeland security.

---

## CERTIFICATION PROGRAMS IN HOMELAND SECURITY

Certification programs are available for those applicants who already have at least a bachelor's degree, and would like to further their education in homeland security without obtaining an additional degree. Numerous colleges and universities offer programs designed to provide education from entry level to advanced training in homeland security. A word of caution—the federal government does not formally recognize any specific homeland security certification course. However, obtaining certification will demonstrate that you have pursued additional knowledge in homeland security issues.

The American College of Forensic Examiners has created the American Board for Certification in Homeland Security (ABCHS). This program offers certifications ranging from Level I (beginner) to Level IV (advanced expert). This program has been endorsed by the Department of Defense and other agencies within the federal government. More information on this program can be obtained by visiting www.abchs.com.

Other colleges and universities offer executive certification programs in homeland security. These programs range in length from several days to a semester in length. Some programs have extensive prerequisites and are designed for those professionals who are already active in executive homeland security roles and responsibilities. Here is a noninclusive list of some of the colleges and universities that are offering graduate-level certification courses in homeland security:

- ▶ Excelsior College
- ▶ Texas A&M University
- ▶ Michigan State University

▶ Saint Joseph University
▶ University of Massachusetts
▶ Post University
▶ Penn State
▶ Long Island University
▶ Southwestern College
▶ Drexel University
▶ Canyon College Eastern Kentucky University
▶ Thomas Edison State College
▶ George Bush School of Government
▶ University of Illinois
▶ San Diego State University
▶ University of Denver
▶ Canyon College (online)

As the future of homeland security continues to evolve, more and more colleges and universities will be developing programs designed to prepare current and future professionals for a career in homeland security. The vast majority of positions within DHS require a college degree, and it is essential that the applicant study the requirements for each position in which they are interested, and make sure that they will have the education required for the position.

With the increasing number of applicants for each position, it is critical that you find different ways to obtain the knowledge and education needed to make you stand out above all the other candidates. Always make sure that the educational program that you are pursuing is accredited and will be recognized by the DHS. If you have any questions or doubts, contact a DHS recruiter prior to starting any program. Do not simply take the college or university's word that their program is accepted by the federal government, as many college recruiters may not be familiar with the educational requirements of the DHS.

# CHAPTER eleven

## FEDERAL RESUMES AND KSAs

**APPLYING FOR** a position with the DHS requires the creation of a federal resume, which is a much more involved process than creating a typical private sector resume. A federal will ask you to go into much further detail than a typical resume, and will also ask for personal information, such as your Social Security number and date of birth.

This chapter highlights important details to help you in the preparation and delivery of the federal resume, and provides you with an overview of the application process, to help make your application for a position with the DHS a little easier.

## GETTING YOUR RESUME STARTED

If you are serious about applying for a position within the DHS, the first step is to familiarize yourself with the federal government's official website, USAJOBS.GOV, which we have already discussed in Chapter 9. Because it is a government website, there is no charge to search for posted jobs, create an account, create a federal resume, store your resume online, or submit to a job announcement.

### QUICK FACT

USAJOBS.GOV provides a free online resume builder that allows you to create up to five different federal resumes, so that you can tailor them to different job applications.

### My Jobs Account

To create a federal resume on USAJOBS.GOV, you must first create a "My Jobs Account." Once you have accomplished that, you can then enter the online resume builder. In the builder you can create up to five separate federal resumes, save your work online, and return to work on it any time and from any place with Internet access. It also offers you the opportunity to update information as needed. You can print a paper copy of your federal resume to send to the DHS when directed by the job announcement, or submit it electronically directly through a job announcement.

## USING THE USAJOBS RESUME BUILDER

The USAJOBS resume builder helps you create your resume by compiling information in a step-by-step process, which can be speeded up significantly by knowing the basics of what you'll be asked for in each step. Following, you'll find a breakdown of the sections you'll need to complete in the USAJOBS resume builder and the information needed for each.

## Confidentiality

Here you can choose whether to hide your contact information, current employer name, and references from recruiters performing resume searches, or display the information.

## Candidate Information

You'll be asked for a resume title, your name, Social Security number, address, and contact information. There are also "yes" or "no" questions pertaining to U.S. citizenship status, veteran's preference, and Selective Service registration.

## Highest Career Level Achieved

In this portion of the builder, you must select the level that most clearly reflects where you are in your career. You'll find a drop-down box with the following choices: Student (High School); Student (College); Entry Level; Experienced (Non-Manager, Manager/Supervisor of Staff); Executive (Senior Vice President, Vice President, Department Head); or Senior Executive (President, Chief Financial Officer, etc.).

## Federal Employee Information

This box asks if you currently are or were ever a federal civilian employee.

## Work Experience

Here you'll enter your relevant work experience. Start with the most recent (including your current employer) and be sure to include the company name of your employer, plus the city, state, ZIP, and country. You'll be asked for titles held, start and end dates of employment, salary, and average hours per week. You will also be asked if the DHS can contact your supervisor, and if this position is a federal position. Following these questions is the box for your Duties, Accomplishments, and Related Skills. Here is where you detail your experience as it relates to the job requirements and standards. To save your information once you complete the Work Experience section, be sure to click "Add Work Experience." You will have an opportunity to go back and add additional work experience later. This section is covered in more detail later in this chapter.

## Education

Particular jobs require specific education requirements, so be sure to include all your schooling here. Add the details of each phase of schooling and remember to click "Add Education" when you have completed the section.

## Related Training

Here you should include seminars, training courses, continuing education, and any other training that relates to the job for which you are applying. Please note that this input box provides room for only 2,000 characters total.

## References

This section is an optional one. Here you enter the contact information for each reference and select whether the reference is professional or personal. Make sure you save each of your references by clicking "Add Reference."

## Additional Language Skills

If you speak, write, or read any additional languages you should include that here. You'll find a drop-down box to select the language and proficiency levels in speaking, writing, and reading. Do not forget to save each addition under "Add Language." Remember, if you indicate that you can speak, read, or write a foreign language, you will most likely be tested to determine your proficiency, so be truthful.

## Affiliations

This is an optional section in which to include relevant affiliations. Enter the organization name, your role, or title. Do not forget to save under "Add Affiliation."

## Professional Publications

This is an optional section in which to include relevant professional publications to which you have contributed.

## Additional Information

In this section you would include any job-related honors, awards, leadership activities, skills, public speaking engagements, or any other information requested by the job announcement. This section is also utilized to enter the KSA (Knowledge, Skills and Abilities) requirements for the particular job announcement. (KSAs are further discussed later in this chapter.)

## Availability

This is an optional section in which to include the types of work you are willing to accept and is used by recruiters searching for candidates. The choices here are: Permanent, Temporary, Term, Intermittent, Detail, Temporary Promotion, Summer, Seasonal, Federal Career Intern, and Student Career Experience. You are also asked here what type of work schedule you would be willing to accept. Your choices are: Full Time, Part Time, Shift Work, Intermittent, and Job Share.

## Looking for a Specific Work Environment

This section, utilized by recruiters, covers where you are in your career. This can range from being a graduating student starting a career with the federal government to retirees from both the private sector and federal service.

## Desired Locations

This section provides recruiters with more information on your desired work location. You have the opportunity to choose a region or specific locations.

Now that you have seen the basic steps needed to prepare a federal resume, let us look at the most important sections you will be filling out while completing the resume builder—the Work Experience sections and KSAs.

## WORK EXPERIENCE SECTION

### QUICK TIP

Be as detailed as you can when describing your work experience. Try to show that your work experience meets the requirements for the job for which you are applying.

The most important section on the USAJOBS.GOV resume builder is the Work Experience section. Here, you have the opportunity to detail your work experience in three different areas—duties, accomplishments, and related skills. You do not have to create your work experience on the USAJOBS.GOV resume builder; you can instead use your favorite writing software and then copy and paste your information into your federal resume online. Just keep in mind that each area has a 3,000 character limit.

The Office of Personnel Management publishes Qualification Standards for every job listed on USAJOBS.GOV on their website at www .opm.gov. As you create your resume, you should refer to these standards to find key words that describe the responsibilities and skills for the position for which you are applying. By doing so you'll be able to relate your experience to the critical skills, specialized experience, and duties required to perform the job at the grade level of the position requirements. Also, study the job announcement for your selected position to relate the competencies required for the job to your own experience. Describe your experience as it relates to the requirements by including your achievements and contributions and make sure you offer examples that illustrate how you meet the specified qualifications. Once you submit your federal resume, a human resource specialist will review it to ensure that it meets the requirements of the Qualification Standards for that position, as well as the job announcement under Duties and Qualifications. Your description in the work experience section must meet these requirements to be considered for the position.

## KNOWLEDGE, SKILLS, AND ABILITIES

Federal hiring laws require all hiring agencies to analyze each job within the agency in order to determine its duties and responsibilities and then to state the knowledge, skills, and abilities required to perform the job effectively. **Knowledge** is defined as the body of information, usually factual or procedural in nature, needed to perform a job function. **Skills** are defined as measurable competencies to perform specific mental, manual, or verbal manipulations. **Abilities** are the competencies to perform observable activities or behaviors that result in observable products, similar to those required in the job.

Those statements of necessary qualifications are called KSAs. The statements you must write in response to the agency KSAs are also called KSAs. The two meanings of the term are used interchangeably.

For most federal jobs, you will be asked to write between three and six KSAs. Some complex jobs may require as many as eight. The ability to write effective KSAs is the single most important skill you need to become a successful job applicant. If your KSAs do not demonstrate that you meet the job requirements, it does not matter how much experience you have or how well-suited you are for the position. You will not get the job. You will not even clear the first hurdle toward getting the job.

Think of the KSAs as pre-interview questions. Analyze each question and formulate the appropriate response as you would do in an interview. Illustrate your life experiences, education, and training as they relate to the questions. Present your KSAs in specific or measurable terms, as in money saved or sales increased. Demonstrate your ability to produce and show responsibility. Use action words or buzzwords to describe your experiences. Use wording found in the job announcement under duties to determine that you meet the requirements for the position. Include all your relevant work experience, not just one job held. Try and limit KSAs to one or one and a half pages in length.

## HOW TO WRITE A KSA

To effectively answer the question found in the KSA, you must first carefully read and understand the KSA. The KSAs tend to be general in nature, so make sure you understand what they are looking for in the question. Read the job description contained in the job announcement. Compare the job description to the KSA question. This will help you relate your answer to the job for which you are applying.

Here are five important components to remember when formulating your KSA answer:

1. Describe specific situations.
2. Give an overview of your experience.
3. Give an example of relevant experience or training.
4. Describe an award for specific accomplishments.
5. Describe a specific experience from a previous job in history format.

Once you understand the question, review your education, training, awards, school related activities, and job skills, including both paid and volunteer experiences that relate to the KSA statement. Start from your earliest experiences and work forward. Do not worry about reusing experiences. Experience may apply to more than one KSA statement. Take the time to review your experiences as they relate to the KSA. Write down examples demonstrating your knowledge, skills, and abilities to do the job for which you are applying.

Once you have identified experiences that relate to the job question, you must analyze each experience individually, asking yourself the following questions.

### What Kind of Knowledge or Skills Do I Use in the Experience?

- What are the steps, procedures, practices, rules, policies, theories, principles, or concepts that my experiences possess?
- How do I apply the knowledge, principles, or concepts utilizing the experience?
- How do I apply knowledge I possess to accomplish this experience?

### What Kind of Supervision Do I Receive?

- How was my experience assigned?
- What was my responsibility to accomplish the task?
- How independent were my actions?
- How was my experience reviewed by superiors?

### What Guidelines Did I Use to Accomplish the Experience?

- Were the instructions utilized in written or oral form, or both?
- Did I use procedural manuals?
- What other written procedures did I use to perform the experience?
- What oral instructions did I use to perform the experience?
- How much judgment did I use to apply the guidelines?
- Were the guidelines easy to apply or did they require me to interpret them?

### How Complex Was the Experience?

- How difficult was the experience process to perform?
- How difficult was it to identify what needed to be accomplished?
- How difficult or original was my experience?

### How Did My Experience Affect Other Processes or Individuals?

- Who did I have contact with on a daily basis?
- Why did I have contact with these individuals?
- What was my role in meetings or discussions?

### QUICK FACT

When writing a KSA, do not use abbreviations or industry specific jargon. The people who initially review your KSA might not have any experience in the field to which you are applying.

Once you have answered these questions as they relate to your experiences, you are ready to show how the facts you have gathered about your experiences relate to the KSA. You must link your experiences and the KSA. The links must be obvious to the person reading your KSA. Your answer is rated on content, not the writing style you utilize, so use short, direct, sentences that get right to the point. When writing, do not use abbreviations, acronyms, or industry jargon. Chances are the person reviewing your KSA would not understand what you are trying to say. The human resources specialist who reviews your application may not be familiar with the position or even the career field. To help the screener, utilize some of the same words that are found in the job announcement, especially words that describe job duties or qualifications.

The KSAs are a very important part of the application process. The ability to effectively communicate is a trait highly sought in the federal government. Specialists and supervisors who review KSAs score your responses based on the following factors: complexity of duties, circumstances, impact, variety, duration, and people contacted.

Now the good news—the federal government is working to eliminate KSAs. In 2008, the Office of Personnel Management called for the elimination of the cumbersome Knowledge, Skills, and Abilities (KSAs) narratives typically required with the federal resume.[1] However, this does not mean that they are entirely gone from the job announcements. Some job announcements require specific knowledge, skills, and abilities, as the hiring personnel need to know if you have what it takes to do the job. These specific questions as they pertain to the job may now be called questionnaires or assessments.

## FEDERAL RESUME COMPLETED?

Once you have completed your federal resume and KSAs, read, reread, and then read them again. You are representing your personal best in this federal resume and spelling errors, punctuation, and grammar could mean the difference between being selected for the position or not. Be critical; how will the person reviewing perceive what you have written? Ask yourself, would I hire me based on what is written here? Did the points I was trying to make appear clear and concise? Have friends, teachers, or contacts that you develop review what you have written. (Developing contacts is discussed in detail in Chapter 13).

### QUICK FACT

It is extremely important to spell check your federal resume and KSAs before you submit them. Errors in spelling, punctuation, and grammar can quickly eliminate you from the selection process.

Once you have reviewed your application, it is time to submit the federal resume. The job announcement contains a tab marked, "How to Apply"; this section provides specifics on what you need to do to apply for the position. Here you will find the types of applications that will be accepted. It contains a description of the necessary information to be included with the application. Pay close attention to the information requested here. You will also find what specific documentation you will be required to include with the application, such as DD-214 Record of Military Service. It also provides the address to which to send your application to be considered as a candidate. It provides the cutoff date of the announcement, and also contains the point of contact for obtaining additional information regarding the vacancy announcement.

## PROFESSIONAL FEDERAL RESUME WRITERS

If you are not confident in your ability to write clearly and eloquently, there are companies that will write your federal resume for you—for a fee. A simple search on the Internet will give you a list of companies that provide this service. Costs range from as little as $50 to hundreds of dollars, based on the complexity of the federal resume and your experience. Word of caution— search for a reputable federal resume writing company, not just price. In a lot of cases, you get what you pay for. Remember, too, that the finished product is only as good as the information you provide. A federal resume writing company will take the information you provide and enhance your experience using key federal buzzwords that job application reviewers or computer search programs are searching for. The use of these buzzwords is based on past successes with other federal resumes. This alternative solution can make a difference in the selection process.

## THE WAITING GAME

The federal resume is a document for starting or advancing your government career. The application that you submit will go through many layers of review before final selection. Upon receipt of your application, human resource specialists will screen it to see if your application meets the basic requirements for the position.

### QUICK FACT

The federal selection process for a position can take months to process. Be prepared to wait after submitting your application.

If it is determined that your application meets the basic requirements, specialists or a panel of experts in the field will rate your application according to the additional qualification requirements listed in the job announcement. If your application rates among the highest, it is forwarded to the hiring manager, who will then choose the winning candidate. Unlike the private sector, the federal application selection process can take months, so be prepared to wait. You can contact the point of contact to determine receipt of your application, and inquire as to the state of the process, but be patient—a future career with the DHS is worth the wait.

# CHAPTER twelve

## OBTAINING A SECURITY CLEARANCE

**MANY OF** the positions within the Department of Homeland Security will require security clearance approval prior to employment. If you are like most other potential applicants, then you probably have several questions about the different levels of security clearances, the security clearance process, and the past actions that may disqualify you from obtaining a clearance.

Not all positions within the DHS will require a security clearance. The scope of the job and the nature of the work will determine whether you will have access to sensitive information during the course of your employment. Let's explore the purpose for security clearances, and the process that you will experience if your particular position requires a security clearance.

The purpose of the security clearance is to determine whether a person is willing and able to safeguard information relating to national security. This determination is based on the person's loyalty to the United States, character, trustworthiness, and reliability.

Obtaining a security clearance is not the same as a preemployment suitability background investigation. A background investigation for security clearance may be conducted by personnel who are not involved in the employment process. However, many positions require approval for appropriate security clearance as a condition of employment.

## QUICK FACT

A security clearance investigation costs the DHS approximately $3,500 to $8,000 per applicant.

Applicants frequently ask whether there is a way to obtain a security clearance prior to applying for a job. Unless someone works for the federal government, or is an approved contractor for the federal government, he or she cannot obtain a security clearance. Individuals cannot determine on their own whether they will need to have a security clearance. Only authorized agencies within the federal government can determine whether individuals need to have access to sensitive information in the course of their duties. It is costly and time-consuming for the federal government to issue security clearances, so only individuals who have been offered employment with the DHS can obtain security clearance. On average, the investigation costs DHS between $3,500 and $8,000 per person depending on the time involved.

A number of agencies within the federal government issue security clearances:

- ▶ The Department of Homeland Security
- ▶ The Department of State
- ▶ The Department of Justice
- ▶ The Department of Energy
- ▶ The Department of Defense
- ▶ The Central Intelligence Agency
- ▶ United States Agency for International Development
- ▶ National Nuclear Security Administration

## QUICK FACT

The Department of Defense accounts for more than 80% of all issued security clearances.

Prospective DHS employees who already have a security clearance with one of these federal agencies will find that they still have to go through an abbreviated background investigation to determine whether there have been any major changes in clearance eligibility. Currently, federal agencies do not have a standard security clearance that is accepted across all branches of government. The Department of Homeland Security may accept prior background investigations done by other federal agencies, as long as the investigation was done within ten years for secret clearances, and within five years for top secret clearances. The investigation must also have been conducted using the 13 Adjudication Guidelines and there must be reciprocal recognition of security clearances between the two agencies involved. For example, a person who has a security clearance as a contractor with the Department of Defense may not automatically be given a clearance with the Department of Homeland Security, since no reciprocal recognition agreement exists between the two agencies.

A security clearance will remain in effect for the duration of employment, unless the employee's job description changes and they no longer require security access. The Department of Homeland Security is also responsible for conducting routine investigations during employees' employment with the DHS to maintain the integrity of their security clearance.

**QUICK FACT**

There are technically only three levels of security clearance that are recognized by DHS: Confidential, Secret, and Top Secret.

## LEVELS OF SECURITY CLEARANCE

There are three primary levels of security clearance:

▶ Confidential
▶ Secret
▶ Top Secret

**Confidential** clearance is issued to personnel who have access to information that reasonably could be expected to cause damage to national security if disclosed to unauthorized sources. Most members of the Department of Defense have this basic level of clearance. Confidential clearance is reinvestigated every 15 years. An example of confidential information would be knowledge that a new, classified intelligence agency called the National Reconnaissance Office has been established. (The existence of the National Reconnaissance Office was classified when it was established in 1961, and was not declassified until 1997.[1])

**Secret** clearance is issued to personnel who have access to information that reasonably could be expected to cause serious damage to national security if disclosed to unauthorized sources. A Secret clearance is reinvestigated every 10 years. An example of secret information would be knowledge that the mission of the National Reconnaissance Office is to build and operate the United States' spy satellites.

**Top Secret** clearance is issued to personnel who have access to information that reasonably could be expected to cause exceptionally grave damage to national security if disclosed to unauthorized sources. A Top Secret clearance is reinvestigated every five years. An example of top secret information would be photos taken by a satellite with the National Reconnaissance Office showing information that could jeopardize national security.

**Top Secret Sensitive Compartmented Information (TS-SCI)** and **Top Secret Special Access Program (TS-SAP)** are technically not levels of security clearance. Sensitive Compartmented Information and Special Access Program are endorsements to a top secret clearance. These levels of clearance do not allow individuals a wide range of access to various types of classified information. Instead, they allow an individual access only to information that is need-to-know. The determination for "need-to-know" and the need for an SCI or SAP clearance are determined by the employer, not the employee. In order to obtain an SCI or SAP clearance, an individual must be nominated for an SCI/SAP billet and then approved following a comprehensive investigation of suitability.

All SCI/SAP clearances are regulated by the Central Intelligence Agency under the Director of Central Intelligence Directive (DCID) Number 6/4. To obtain a TS-SCI or TS-SAP clearance, an individual must submit to an extensive background investigation, which usually includes a comprehensive polygraph examination to determine suitability for clearance. If an individual already has top secret clearance and is receiving an SCI/SAP clearance, it normally takes three to six months to complete the process. Individuals with no prior security clearance who are being issued a TS-SCI or TS-SAP clearance should expect at least one year for the approval process unless there exists an unusual and emergent need for their skill or expertise.

Other branches of government may have specific levels of clearances (such as the Department of Energy, which has an L level clearance that is equivalent to a confidential or secret clearance, and a Q level clearance which is equivalent to a top secret clearance). However, only the three basic levels of clearance are recognized across the span of the federal government.

A security clearance does not automatically give an individual an "all access pass" to information. For example, a person with top secret clearance cannot access all information that is classified as top secret. The person must have a bona fide need to know the information. There are multiple safeguards throughout the federal government to prevent unauthorized access to classified information. As a general rule of thumb, the Department of Homeland Security will actively work to reduce the number of clearances whenever possible to minimize the risk of accidental or intentional dissemination of information.

## THE SECURITY CLEARANCE PROCESS

The security clearance investigation is extremely comprehensive and involves checking the applicant's name against a variety of agencies, including the following.

The **Defense Central Index of Investigations (DCII)** is a comprehensive automated central index that identifies investigations conducted by the Department of Defense and Department of Defense contractors. The DCII will be checked to see whether the applicant has been the subject of a previous security clearance investigation, and the disposition of the investigation.

The **Federal Bureau of Investigation Headquarters (FBI-HQ)** maintains a copy of all federal investigations conducted by the FBI. The FBI-HQ database will be referenced to see whether the applicant has ever been the subject of an investigation in which the FBI participated. The Federal Bureau of Investigation Identification (FBI/ID) Unit will check to see whether the applicant has been the subject of a fingerprint search by a law enforcement agency as part of a criminal investigation. The FBI also maintains a comprehensive record of fingerprints that have been obtained by local, state, and federal law enforcement agencies throughout the United States.

The **Office of Personnel Management (OPM)** contains the results of any investigation that has been conducted by the OPM or the Department of Energy (DOE) since 1952. OPM is the lead agency for issuing security clearances for civilian employees of the United States government, U.S. citizens who have been employed by the United Nations or other public international organizations, and any individual who has been granted a security clearance by the Nuclear Regulatory Commission (NRC) or the DOE.

**Immigration and Naturalization Services (INS)** maintains a comprehensive file of the following: naturalization certificates, certificates of derivative citizenship, military certificates of naturalization, repatriation files, petitions for naturalization and declaration of intention, visitor visas, and records of aliens admitted into the United States. Immigration and Naturalization Services' records will be checked if the applicant is an immigrant alien or a United States citizen who receives derivative citizenship through the naturalization of one or both parents. It is important to note that nonresidents of the United States are rarely granted a security clearance. Security clearance is granted only to nonresidents who possess very specialized skill, when there are no available United States citizens who possess the same skill.

The **State Department** maintains a record of all individuals who have been investigated for any violation of national security since 1950. The Passport Division (P/D) of the State Department is also checked if the applicant has indicated United States citizenship due to birth in a foreign country of American parents. This situation is frequently encountered during security clearances if the applicant was born outside of the United States to parents who were serving in the United States military. In cases such as these, the Department of Defense will be contacted as well to corroborate the parent's tour of duty outside the country when the applicant was born.

The **Central Intelligence Agency (CIA) Office of the Directorate of Operations (CIA-DO/IMS)** maintains a comprehensive database on foreign intelligence and counterintelligence. This database will be checked to see whether the individual has ever been listed as a counterintelligence risk for the United States. The Central Intelligence Agency Office of Security (CIA-SEC) maintains information on all present and former employees, including members of the Office of Strategic Services (OSS) and all applicants for employment. All records will be checked to see whether the CIA can offer any pertinent information about the applicant.

The **United States Military Personnel Record Center** maintains all files of current and former members of the U.S. Armed Forces. If the applicant is retired, separated, active duty or reserve, the Military Personnel Record Center will be contacted and information will be obtained on the applicant.

The **United States Treasury Department**, including the **Secret Service (USSS)**, **Internal Revenue Service (IRS)**, and the **Bureau of Customs** will be checked for information about the applicant. The Department of Treasury may be requested to search automated databases consisting of reports of currency transactions by financial institutions to see whether there is a history of the applicant receiving or transmitting large amounts of money that could indicate criminal activity. Applicants will frequently have to answer questions that arise from the IRS including failure to pay taxes, current tax arrears, and any garnishment of wages. An applicant who has experienced any of these needs to be prepared to settle the matter with the IRS, write an explanation, and have a letter from the IRS indicating that the matter has been successfully resolved.

The **International Criminal Police Organization (INTERPOL)** will be contacted if the applicant:

▶ has maintained non-military foreign residence in excess of six months
▶ has engaged in non-military employment overseas in excess of six months
▶ has engaged in academic activities abroad in excess of six months
▶ admits to being the subject of a criminal investigation while outside of the United States

And finally, the **Bureau of Vital Statistics** may be contacted if there are any discrepancies regarding the applicant's birth certificate, or to corroborate the date and place of birth.

## THE STANDARD FORM 86 AND e-QIP

Candidates for security clearance must first fill out the Standard Form 86 (SF-86), which is an application for security clearance. The SF-86 is a 19-page form that asks a variety of questions regarding a person's background. It is now located online, and the form is filled out electronically through the Office of Personnel Management's (OPM) website. A candidate who is asked to fill out the form using the OPM website will be given a username and password to access the electronic form using a program called e-QIP. With their username and password, an applicant can work on the form and save the work without having to submit the form. Once the SF-86 is completed, the candidate electronically locks the form, and then submits it through e-QIP. The form will then be sent electronically to the authorized representative with the Department of Homeland Security. The candidate will also have to print several signature pages, and submit them via mail to their employment recruiter at the DHS along with any requested supporting documentation.

If candidates realize that they omitted information after they have submitted the form electronically, they will need to contact their individual recruiters to have them unlock the form. It is not uncommon to have the form unlocked one or two times to have candidates fill in additional information, but candidates should strive to have the form filled out completely prior to submission so that it does not have to be unlocked. If the form has to be repeatedly unlocked to allow the candidate to fill in information, it may lead to a decision not to hire the candidate because he or she cannot follow directions.

Candidates should expect to spend several hours filling out the SF-86. A secret clearance will require the candidate to go back seven years, while a top secret clearance will require the candidate to go back ten years. There are many positions within the DHS that will require the candidate to go back to the age of 18, even if it is greater than ten years in the past. Prior to starting the SF-86, a candidate will need to have a variety of information available for the appropriate requested timeframe, including:

▶ all previous addresses where the candidate has lived
▶ all employers (this includes part-time, full-time and contract employers)

- ▶ date of birth, Social Security number, place of birth, citizenship status of immediate family members
- ▶ United States passport number
- ▶ citizenship or naturalization certificate number
- ▶ addresses of all schools since high school, including attendance dates
- ▶ military records, including units and position titles
- ▶ selective service number (for males)
- ▶ three personal references
- ▶ spousal/cohabitant information (place of birth, citizenship status, date of birth, Social Security number)
- ▶ foreign contacts
- ▶ foreign activities
- ▶ foreign business or contact with foreign governments
- ▶ foreign countries visited
- ▶ mental and emotional heath
- ▶ criminal record
- ▶ illegal use of drugs or drug activity
- ▶ alcohol use
- ▶ previous security clearances and background investigations
- ▶ financial record
- ▶ use of information technology systems
- ▶ involvement in noncriminal court actions
- ▶ association with organizations against the United States government

The SF-86 requires a lot of information and it is not uncommon for the form to exceed 50 or 60 pages. In order to expedite the time that it will take to complete the application, candidates should download the form from the Office of Personnel Management's website and begin filling it out so that it will be ready when it is requested.

## POLYGRAPH

Not all security clearances will require a polygraph. However, a lot of positions within the DHS that require a secret or top secret clearance will require a polygraph during the preemployment phase. Depending on the nature of the top secret clearance, a candidate may be required to submit to a polygraph. An example of this includes personnel who are obtaining a top secret clearance for the purpose of working in counterterrorism or counterintelligence. If candidates are required to submit to a polygraph, they will only be questioned about information provided on the SF-86.

## INVESTIGATION OF FAMILY MEMBERS, SPOUSE, AND COHABITANT

Under certain circumstances, a limited background investigation may be conducted on a spouse or cohabitant of individuals being processed for a top secret clearance. A more detailed background investigation may be conducted if the spouse or cohabitant is a foreign national. A cohabitant is defined as someone with whom an applicant resides and the relationship involves the mutual assumption of marital-type rights, duties, and obligations that would normally be manifested by married people. The definition of cohabitation is independent of sexual relations between the two individuals.

An ex-spouse will be contacted as part of the investigation as long as the divorce has been less than ten years. If the divorce occurred because of domestic violence or criminal activity, then the ex-spouse will be contacted regardless of the timeframe.

## THE ADJUDICATION PROCESS

The adjudication process is an examination of the candidate's SF-86 and the results of the background investigation. The process is designed to ensure that the candidate will not be a security risk, and can be trusted with sensitive information. The adjudication process uses the whole-person concept. This means that the adjudicators look at all available information, determine reliability of the information, look at the source of the information, and then weigh the favorable factors against the unfavorable factors in order to reach a final determination. The adjudicators do not expect candidates to be perfect and understand that people make mistakes.

When the adjudicators review an applicant's background, they will make a determination of the applicant's conduct based on several factors. First, they will look at the nature, extent, and seriousness of the conduct. They will also look at the circumstances surrounding the conduct. Applicants must realize that participation in immoral, unethical, or illegal action will be carefully scrutinized. Not only is participation reviewed, but if the applicant had knowledge of immoral, unethical, or illegal actions and did not act appropriately, he or she can be considered guilty by association. The adjudicators will also look at the frequency of the conduct, including how recently it was last conducted. Adjudicators understand that people make mistakes. However, people who repeatedly make the same mistakes are showing a pattern that will probably continue.

Adjudicators will also look at the applicant's age and maturity at the time of the conduct. Depending on the seriousness of the behavior, the adjudicators may ask for a detailed explanation of the behavior, including the reasons why the applicant will not make the same mistakes. Adjudicators will also ask about the motivation for the conduct. Adjudicators may be more understanding of past behavior if there was a compelling reason for the conduct.

As the adjudicators look at all the information, they will also want to know whether the applicant has engaged in any specific behavior modifications to prevent that type of behavior in the future. These behavior modifications may include counseling, support groups, or significant behavior changes. For example, if an applicant had an arrest for driving while intoxicated when in college, the adjudicators would want to know if the applicant attended any type of alcohol treatment program. Court-ordered treatment will not be viewed as favorably as applicant-initiated treatment.

Once the adjudicators analyze the behavioral information they must make two very important determinations. First, they must determine whether the applicant's behavior will be continued after they are employed and have a security clearance. If the adjudicators believe that the behavior will be continued, they will be hesitant to authorize a security clearance. Second, the adjudicators must look at the applicant's potential for coercion, exploitation, or duress if someone else were to come into possession of their background information. For example, if an applicant has had an extramarital affair and his or her spouse does not know about the affair, the applicant could be pressured or blackmailed to give up information in exchange for not giving information about the affair to the spouse. Unfortunately, extramarital affairs are common, and frequently come up in background investigations. The adjudicators may want proof that the spouse is aware of all the details of the affair so that there is no potential for blackmail; this would include interviewing the spouse about the affair.

If the adjudicators find a pattern of questionable judgment and dishonest, immoral, unethical or unstable behavior, there stands a good chance that the applicant will be denied clearance. The adjudicators will forward their findings to the Department of Homeland Security, which makes the final decision. If there is any doubt as to whether the applicant may pose a threat to national security, the applicant will not be granted any form of security clearances.

### QUICK FACT

At any given time, there are over 350,000 current or prospective employees waiting for a security clearance.

## SECURITY CLEARANCE PROCESS TIMEFRAME

The typical secret security clearance takes an average of 120 days to complete. A top secret security clearance takes an average of one year to complete; however, applicants should expect it to take even longer based on the security clearance case load. According to the Defense Industrial Security Clearance Office, the average top secret application processing period is 111 days, the investigation period averages 286 days, and the adjudication process averages 39 days.[2] Applications that are filled out incompletely can take up to two and a half years to complete.

### QUICK FACT

The typical secret security clearance investigation takes an average of 120 days to complete. A top secret security clearance investigation takes an average of one year to complete.

If an applicant has a prior security clearance through another agency, a small portion of the new investigation will not have to be repeated. However, applicants should expect the usual wait time to obtain a security clearance with DHS. Applicants who have other immediate family members who have security clearances will not see expedited times with their security clearance process.

There are several reasons why it takes a long time to obtain a security clearance. For over a decade, the federal government has allotted insufficient resources to processing security clearances. Because of this, a large number of applications have stacked up, causing a significant delay in processing new requests. Currently, over three million employees in the federal government require some form of security clearance. At any given time, there are over 350,000 current or prospective employees waiting for security clearance.

Secondary to the lack of federal resources, there are several factors that can cause delays by the applicant. One of the most common causes of delay occurs when an applicant does not accurately complete the SF-86. The instructions on filling out the application must be followed exactly as stated. Failure to complete the application will result in significant processing delays, as it must be sent back to the applicant to be redone correctly.

Some of the more common problems with the SF-86 include the following: incorrect or out-of-date addresses or phone numbers, lapses of time in the sections labeled "Where You Lived" and "Where You Worked," and inconsistencies between the "Where You Lived" and "Where You Worked" sections. The path of least resistance concept is sometimes used when background investigators conduct security clearances. With the tremendous backlog of security clearances pending, a background investigator may be given multiple cases to work on at the same time. Naturally, the background investigator will complete the easiest background investigations first. These include applications that have been completely and accurately submitted, and applicants who have not moved many times or held multiple jobs. The background investigators do not know the applicants personally, so to them each application is just a file to close. The easier the file is to close, the quicker it will be done. Difficult files may continue to get pushed to the back as easier files come in. It naturally makes sense that an investigator would choose to complete three easy files in the time that it takes to do one difficult file.

Incorrect or out-of-date addresses or phone numbers will significantly slow down the investigative process. Although it is the investigator's responsibility to conduct a background investigation, it is not his or her responsibility to track down old addresses and phone numbers for the applicant. Also, the applicant has a significantly more vested interest in having the background completed on time then does the investigator.

The applicant needs to account for all time during the required background period. Failing to account for even one month of residency on the application may place the complete file on hold. This frequently happens when applicants forget to list residency during college. Applicants who attended a college out of state while maintaining a residency at their parents' house or held a job in one state while they resided in another state must show that they were commuting the whole time. All the time in the investigation has to be accounted for in the "Where You Lived" section and the "Where You Worked" section. Any inconsistency between the two sections is also a frequent cause for delays.

A second reason for delays in processing a security clearance occurs when an applicant has spent an extended period of time outside the United States for residency, business, or pleasure. Applicants who have traveled to countries that are not allies of the United States will face an even longer delay while their purpose for travel is carefully scrutinized.

Another common reason that results in a delay in processing the clearance is a failure of the candidate to obtain a proper set of fingerprints. When the clearance investigation is initiated, the applicant will be given two sets of fingerprint cards that must be completed. The cards are usually taken to the local police department where the fingerprints can be obtained for a minor fee. Both sets of fingerprint cards must be completely and accurately filled out and submitted with the clearance application.

## QUICK FACT

Lying on a federal employment application or security clearance application can have grave consequences, including termination from employment, criminal charges, and a lifetime ban on employment with the federal government.

Lastly, applicants who have serious security or suitability issues will experience a significant delay in the processing of their applications while their backgrounds are thoroughly investigated. Applicants who are believed to have lied on any portion of their applications will have careful attention accorded to the rest of their application, causing significant delays. Lying on an employment application or security application is not only the quickest way to be denied the job, but a way to also be labeled unsuitable for any similar work within the federal government.

## REASONS FOR DENIAL OF CLEARANCE

There are various reasons why an individual may be denied a security clearance. The primary reason is because an individual has either deliberately lied or failed to disclose the truth on the security clearance forms.

Individuals will be denied a clearance when they show evidence of a history of being unreliable or untrustworthy, or evidence of not being completely truthful on the security clearance application (either by acts of commission or acts of omission—that is, deliberately lying or deliberately leaving out important information).

One of the primary reasons for denial of a security clearance lies deep within the disqualifiers discussed in the following pages. In the section of the 13 Steps for Adjudication entitled Concern Regarding Emotional, Mental and Personality Disorder, one of the disqualifiers occurs when the security investigation provides information that suggests that the individual's current behavior indicates a defect in his or her judgment or reliability. This is a caveat catchall. If the adjudicators feel that the applicant has not been completely forthright with information in the background investigation, the adjudicators may cite this as the primary disqualifier for a security clearance.

The following are the 13 key areas that are investigated when determining security clearance suitability.[3]

## CONCERN REGARDING ALLEGIANCE TO THE UNITED STATES

If an applicant is going to have access to information or material that could pose a threat to national security, he or she must have an unwavering, indisputable allegiance to the United States. If there is any information that may question this allegiance, then the applicant may be denied a clearance. Behavior and actions that will pose a security risk, and will result in denial of clearance are:

- ▶ Behavior that demonstrates a significant risk for security includes any involvement in acts of sabotage, espionage, treason, terrorism, sedition, or any other act whose aim was to overthrow the government of the United States, or to coerce or alter the government by any means other than those allowed in the United States Constitution. Anyone who has a history of involvement in any of those behaviors will not be considered for any type of security clearance.
- ▶ Applicants who associate with, or demonstrate sympathy for, a person or group attempting to commit sabotage, espionage, treason, terrorism, sedition, or any acts of violence against the government of the United States (encompassing any division of the Government to include local and state agencies).

An applicant may be considered for a clearance if he or she was involved with individuals or an organization that proposed to commit harm against the government, but was unaware of the unlawful aims of those people or that organization and immediately severed ties with them upon learning of their purpose. However, the applicant will have to prove that the individual or organization's desire to commit harm to the government was not readily available knowledge. It would be very hard for individuals to say that they worked in the office of the ecoterrorist group Earth Liberation Front (ELF), but had no knowledge of the organization's intent to commit illegal activities. Applicants who can demonstrate that their involvement occurred only for a short period of time, and was attributed to curiosity or academic interest, may still be eligible for a security clearance. One of the main deciding factors will be the length of time these individuals spent with the organization, their activity within the organization, and the length of time separating them from the involvement of association of such activities.

## FOREIGN INFLUENCE

It is critical to determine whether an applicant will be a security risk because of the potential for foreign influence. There exists a significant potential if the applicant has immediate family members or cohabitants who are not citizens of the United States. The adjudicators will attempt to determine whether the family member/cohabitant relationship is influenced by affection, or any other type of obligation that may put the applicant in a position where they could be vulnerable to compromise. Applicants who have significant contacts with foreign citizens will also be carefully scrutinized. Applicants will also need to report any family members who had, or currently have, any association with foreign governments. Applicants may pose a significant security risk if their family members or any cohabitant with the applicant currently works for a foreign government, especially in military or intelligence roles. If the applicant has financial interests (such as ownership in a foreign business), they may be viewed as being especially vulnerable to foreign influence.

Applicants can help to ease the security concerns if they can demonstrate that their immediate family members, cohabitants, or other associates are not agents of a foreign country and that they will not be put in any position where they would be vulnerable to sharing information. Applicants would also be able to minimize security concerns if they can prove that their contact with foreign nationals is on behalf of official U.S. government business. If the contact is not on behalf of the government, applicants may need to prove that the contact is infrequent and casual in nature. Applicants who have financial interests in a foreign country will need to demonstrate that their financial interests are not significant enough to pose a security threat. Cases such as these will be reviewed on an individual basis to determine the extent of involvement and potential for risk.

## FOREIGN PREFERENCE

An applicant's allegiance to the United States is of paramount importance. The adjudicators will want to make sure that the applicant does not have any known or potential allegiance to another nation. Potential issues that could disqualify an applicant include maintaining dual citizenship, possession of a foreign passport, or serving with another nation's military. If the applicant has received significant benefits from another country including tuition reimbursement, medical benefits, retirement income or welfare, he or she might not qualify for a clearance. Applicants who have resided in a foreign country (with exceptions for military, official U.S. government business, missionary work, or education), will need to fully explain the purpose of living outside the United States. Applicants who have ever held a political office, voted in foreign elections, or assisted political parties outside of the United States will most likely be denied a clearance. Applicants who have attempted to perform any official government duties for nations outside of the United States will be suspected of having a significant foreign preference.

Applicants can assist the adjudicators with addressing these concerns if they can prove that they had dual citizenship because of a parent's citizenship or because of their birth in a foreign country. If they still maintain a dual citizenship, they will need to be prepared to renounce their citizenship status with any nation other than the United States. Applicants who have foreign military service or worked for a foreign government will need to prove that it occurred before they obtained United States citizenship.

## SEXUAL BEHAVIOR

It is important to note that that federal government respects an individual's right to privacy. The government is not in the business of learning each individual's sexual behavior, or sexual preferences. However, behaviors that could put the applicant at risk for coercion, or that define a behavior of deviance or criminal sexual behavior, must be addressed. At no time may sexual preference be used as a determining factor for a security clearance.

### QUICK FACT

The federal government is prohibited from using a person's sexual preference as a factor for determining security clearance suitability.

The adjudicators are looking to determine that the sexual behavior does not indicate a pattern of a personality or emotional disorder. Any behavior that appears to be consistent, ongoing, or compulsive in nature will be addressed.

The following sexual behaviors raise significant security concerns and may be a reason for denial of clearance.

▶ Any sexual behavior that is criminal in nature, whether or not the individual was prosecuted. For example, an applicant was 19 and having sexual relations with a 16-year-old. If he was charged with statutory rape, but the victim's parents refused to press charges, he will still be considered ineligible for a security clearance unless there are significant extenuating circumstances that could explain the behavior.

▶ Any compulsive or addictive sexual behavior where the applicant is unable to stop a pattern of self-destructive or high-risk behavior could jeopardize the applicant's ability to obtain a clearance. For example, applicants may be asked whether they view pornographic websites. If they answer yes, they may be asked the frequency of the visits to the sites. Although viewing the sites may be completely legal, repetitive viewing may indicate a compulsive personality disorder.

▶ Another reason for denial of clearance can be any sexual behavior that may cause the individual to be vulnerable to coercion, exploitation, or duress. For example, an applicant who had an extramarital affair that their spouse does not know about could be at risk for coercion. The adjudicators will want proof that the affair has ended, and that all parties involved are aware of the affair. If the applicant had an affair with another married individual, both of their spouses would have to be made aware of the affair.

▶ Still another reason for denial of clearance is any sexual behavior that is of a public nature and may reflect a lack of discretion or judgment. For example, if any individual is a prominent member of a swinger's club, the behavior may be completely legal. However, it is of a public nature, and may place the applicant at significant risk for coercion. Someone may attempt to infiltrate the club to develop a sexual relationship with the applicant with the sole purpose of gaining access to classified information.

The applicant can take several steps to mitigate the concerns regarding sexual behavior. The applicant needs to be up-front regarding any concerns and be willing to address them completely. The applicant can also mitigate concerns by showing that the behavior occurred during adolescence, and that the behavior has not been continued in adulthood. The applicant can also show that there has been no such recent behavior or similar conduct. The applicant can also demonstrate to the adjudicators that the behavior did not involve questionable judgment, emotional instability, or any irresponsibility. It is important to note that the adjudicators may request a full psychological evaluation of the applicant by a licensed mental health practitioner to address any concerns. The applicant will also have to satisfactorily demonstrate that the behavior cannot be used for coercion or exploitation of the applicant.

## EMOTIONAL, MENTAL, AND PERSONALITY DISORDERS

The Department of Homeland Security does not discriminate against applicants, including those with mental or psychological conditions. However, the DHS has to take due diligence to make sure that the mental illness, emotional illness, or psychological condition will not pose a threat to national security. The adjudicators have to ensure that the applicant will not be predisposed to have a lack of judgment, reliability, or stability.

Applicants will be required to report any mental health counseling they have had. This includes family and marital counseling. The applicant will be required to provide copies of all medical records from any mental health professional who has treated the applicant. The Department of Homeland Security will also require that the applicant be evaluated by a credentialed and licensed mental health professional who is approved by the government. This is frequently paid for by the applicant.

Specific concerns regarding the applicant's suitability for a security clearance include any of the following.

▶ If, in the opinion of a licensed mental health professional, the applicant has a condition that may indicate the potential for errors in judgment, reliability, or stability he or she will not be eligible for a clearance. It is important to note that simply receiving treatment for a condition may not be sufficient to obtain clearance. The concern lies with the potential for the applicant to stop receiving treatment and become a security risk. An example would include a patient who has a severe obsessive-compulsive disorder. The patient's illness may be effectively managed through daily medications, but if the patient were to stop taking the medications, the disease would be debilitating. In cases like this, the applicant may be denied a security clearance because of the potential risk for the applicant to be significantly affected by the illness.

▶ Another significant security concern occurs when the patient has failed to follow a recommended treatment regimen for a specific illness. This may include failure to take prescribed medications, or to attend counseling as advised by a mental health professional.

▶ Applicants who display a pattern of high-risk, irresponsible, aggressive, antisocial, or emotionally unstable behavior may pose a significant risk to national security. For example, an applicant who has had to repeatedly go to sexual harassment training at the workplace because of his or her behavior will most likely be considered a security risk.

▶ If the background investigation, or the evaluation by a mental health professional, provides information that suggests that the individual's current behavior indicates a defect in judgment or reliability, the applicant will not be considered for a security clearance. This is a caveat catchall. If the adjudicators feel that the applicant has not been completely forthright with information in the background investigation, the adjudicators will cite this as the primary disqualifier for a security clearance.

Applicants can mitigate the concerns regarding their emotional, mental, or personality disorders if they can show that there is no indication of a current problem. They can also help to mitigate concerns if they can demonstrate that the disorder was the result of a temporary condition such as a divorce, death, illness, and such. For example, if a patient was treated for depression, but showed that it occurred after the death of a spouse, the adjudicators will recognize that there is little security risk.

Lastly, the applicant can ease concerns if a licensed mental health professional states that in his or her opinion, the disorder is cured, is completely under control, or has a low probability of recurrence.

## PERSONAL CONDUCT

One of the most important aspects of the security clearance investigation is the applicant's ability to be forthright and honest about all concerns. The applicant poses a significant security risk if there is evidence that the applicant lacks candor, has questionable judgment, is dishonest, or is unwilling to comply with rules and regulations.

### QUICK FACT

One of the most important aspects of the security clearance investigation is the applicant's honesty, candor, and forthrightness during the investigation.

The two following circumstances will result in denial of security clearance and immediate termination of the clearance process. (1) If applicants refuse to undergo any required security processing, they will be dismissed from the clearance process. This can include any medical or psychological testing that is required of the applicant. (2) Applicants will be denied clearance if they refuse to complete required security forms, or fail to provide full, truthful answers to questions by the security clearance investigators or other official representatives of the DHS. It is very important to clarify a point here. The background investigator is not looking for a full confession of all wrongdoing by the applicant. Many a candidate has been dismissed for offering up information that otherwise would have never been brought up in the investigation. However, if an applicant is deliberate about attempting to downplay concerns, or hide additional information, they will be viewed as a security risk because of their failure to be candid and frank with the answers.

If the security clearance investigation reveals consistent and reliable unfavorable information about the applicant, there will be significant concerns about the applicant's suitability for a security clearance. This information may come from associates, employers, coworkers, neighbors, and other acquaintances. A frequent question asked by applicants concerns the information that an ex-spouse may provide the background investigator. The investigators know that they will be given information that is not favorable for the applicant. The investigation would not be complete if the investigator did not uncover at least some unfavorable information. However, the investigators and the adjudicators are very aware that some people may provide information about the applicant that is not completely true, simply because they do not like the applicant. If investigators uncover unfavorable information, they will attempt to corroborate it. If they cannot corroborate the information, it will still be given to the adjudicators, but will either be dismissed or regarded as being of little significance.

## FINANCIAL CONSIDERATIONS

Applicants who have demonstrated that they have financial problems, or exhibit behavior that could lead to financial problems (such as clearly living beyond their means) can pose a security risk. The concern is that the individual would be tempted to conduct illegal activities to generate money, or will be subject to external influence to provide information in exchange for money.

**QUICK FACT**

Individuals who have defaulted on a government-backed student loan are ineligible for employment with the federal government.

The following are conditions that raise a significant concern for security and are likely to lead to denial of clearance: The applicant who has a history of being unable to meet financial obligations, such as a history of late payment on bills, will be carefully scrutinized. An applicant who has a history of embezzlement, employee theft, check fraud, income tax evasion, expense account fraud, deceptive loan statements, or any other intentional breach of trust will be considered a security risk. Applicants who have a history of writing worthless checks will be required to provide explanations of the incidents. The adjudicators understand that occasionally someone may bounce a check, but if the applicant is frequently bouncing checks, it will be seen as malicious writing of worthless checks.

An applicant who is unable or unwilling to satisfy any outstanding debts may not be issued a security clearance. This is why it is so important for applicants to get copies of their credit reports prior to applying for a security clearance, so that they can clear up any outstanding credit issues.

If the applicant has demonstrated unexplained affluence—that is, significant monetary support that is coming from a source outside of their immediate family—he or she will be carefully investigated.

Any individual with a history of gambling, drug abuse, alcoholism, or other issues that relate to their finances will be carefully investigated to determine his or her security suitability.

Applicants can help to address the concerns regarding their financial suitability by demonstrating that any questionable financial behavior has not occurred recently, or was an isolated incident. Applicants can also mitigate problems if they can demonstrate that their financial concerns resulted from a situation that was largely beyond their control, such as death of family member, divorce, separation, loss of employment, business downturn, or an unexpected medical condition. Applicants who had outstanding debts on their credit report can also demonstrate that they have made a good faith attempt to resolve all outstanding credit issues. A common example occurs when applicants have an outstanding balance to a creditor who has since gone out of business. There is no way to successfully remove this outstanding balance from a credit report, but they can demonstrate that they have attempted unsuccessfully to resolve the debt.

Applicants who receive money that results in unexplained affluence will need to demonstrate that the money was obtained legally. Applicants who had a history of gambling will need to demonstrate that they have received counseling for the problem, and that it is clearly under control.

## ALCOHOL CONSUMPTION

Applicants who desire a security clearance cannot have a history of excessive alcohol consumption. There are several concerns regarding alcohol use that could make the applicant a security risk. People who have trouble controlling alcohol use are displaying an impulsive behavior that can put them at risk for questionable judgment, lack of self-control, and unreliable behavior.

People who cannot control their alcohol use are at risk for disclosing classified information, or other impulsive behavior.

The following are significant concerns regarding alcohol use, and may result in the applicant's denial of a security clearance: Applicants who have a history of any work-related alcohol incidents, such as reporting for work under the influence or drinking on the job. Applicants who have had any alcohol-related incidents away from work including any of the following—driving while intoxicated, domestic violence, assaults while under the influence, public intoxication, or any other criminal offense related to alcohol. Applicants may be a potential security risk if they have been diagnosed by a licensed medical professional for alcohol abuse or alcohol dependence, or have been evaluated and/or received treatment in an alcohol abuse or alcohol dependence program. It is important to note that a significant disqualifier exists when individuals have consumed alcohol after completing an alcohol rehabilitation program. Applicants may be a potential security risk if they have any other history of habitual or binge consumption of alcohol that would indicate an ongoing condition that could lead to impaired judgment.

The applicant can help to mitigate the concerns by proving that the alcohol-related incidents were isolated, and that no pattern of abuse is present. The applicant can also help to mitigate any concerns by proving that the alcohol-related incidences occurred a number of years in the past and that there is no indication to reflect a current problem. Applicants who have had a problem with alcohol will need to prove that they have made significant positive changes in their behavior or that they have completed an approved inpatient or outpatient alcohol rehabilitation program. In addition, the applicant will need to prove that he or she has abstained from alcohol for a minimum of 12 months, and has received a favorable diagnosis or evaluation from a licensed medical professional indicating that the problem has been successfully resolved.

## DRUG USE

It is obvious that illegal or improper drug use can raise significant concerns about the applicant's ability to maintain and protect classified information. The Department of Homeland Security is well aware that individuals may have experimented with drugs during their adolescence and will attempt to work with applicants to understand their purpose for using illegal drugs, or using legal drugs in an improper manner.

For the purpose of clarification, the term *drugs* refers to any drug that is listed in the Controlled Substance Act of 1970. There are numerous drugs listed in this act, but some of the more commonly abused drugs are listed here:

- ▶ gamma-hydroxybutyric acid (GHB)
- ▶ marijuana
- ▶ heroin
- ▶ opium and any opiates used for pain relief
- ▶ MDMA (Ecstasy)
- ▶ psilocybin (the active ingredient in psychedelic mushrooms)
- ▶ lysergic acid diethylamide (LSD)
- ▶ peyote
- ▶ mescaline
- ▶ methaqualone (quaalude)
- ▶ anabolic steroids
- ▶ benzylpiperazine (BZP, similar to MDMA)
- ▶ cocaine
- ▶ methylphenidate (Ritalin and Concerta)
- ▶ methadone
- ▶ oxycodone
- ▶ fentanyl
- ▶ morphine
- ▶ mixed amphetamine salts (Adderall)
- ▶ dextroamphetamine (Dexedrine)
- ▶ hydromorphine (Dilaudid)
- ▶ codeine
- ▶ hydrocodone with a dose more than 15 mg per dose unit
- ▶ pethidine (Meperidine or Demerol)
- ▶ phencyclidine (PCP)
- ▶ barbiturates
- ▶ amphetamines

- ketamine
- benzodiazepines (such as Valium)
- modafinil (Provigil)
- inhalants
- amyl nitrate ("poppers")

If applicants have any questions about whether they have used a drug that is specified in the Controlled Substance Act of 1970, they need to relay their concerns to their background investigators. Drugs that are classified as cannabis, depressants, narcotics, stimulants, or hallucinogens are most likely listed in the Controlled Substance Act of 1970.

The following will raise significant concerns regarding the applicant's suitability for a security clearance and will most likely result in denial of clearance.

- any applicant with a conviction for illegal drug possession, including cultivation, processing, manufacture, purchase, sale, or distribution
- any applicant who has been diagnosed by a licensed medical professional as having a drug abuse problem or drug dependence condition
- failure to successfully complete a drug treatment program ordered by the judicial system or prescribed by a licensed health care professional
- any applicant with a history of drug use while maintaining a previous security clearance will be denied clearance.

It is crucial to note that most applicants will not make it to the security clearance process if they have significant drug issues in their past—they are frequently weeded out by this point. The Federal Bureau of Investigation lists several criteria that are disqualifications for employment that have also been adopted by the Department of Homeland Security. These are:

- illegal drug (including anabolic steroids) use other than marijuana in the past ten years, or applicants who have engaged in more than minimal experimentation in their lifetime
- use of marijuana within the past three years, or extensive use of marijuana over a substantial period of time

▶ any history of selling drugs for profit, whether there was a criminal investigation or conviction or not

▶ any use of illegal drugs while in a law enforcement position, prosecutorial position, or any position of public trust or public responsibility[4]

Applicants can mitigate concerns over their drug use if they can prove the following: the drug involvement was not recent, it was an isolated event, there is no intent to abuse drugs in the future, satisfactory completion of an approved drug treatment program with no recurrence of abuse and a favorable diagnosis from a licensed medical professional.

## CRIMINAL CONDUCT

Any crimes the applicant has committed will be evaluated to see if there is a pattern of criminal activity that would lead to the suspicion that the applicant has a lack of judgment, reliability, or trustworthiness. The applicant will be asked about any criminal activities that he or she has committed, not just activities that were investigated or criminal activities that lead to formal charges.

### QUICK FACT

Most applicants who have had a felony conviction are ineligible to obtain security clearance.

Any applicant who has committed a single serious crime (such as a felony) or multiple lesser crimes (such as misdemeanors) may be found unsuitable for security clearance. To mitigate the concerns regarding their activities, the applicant will need to prove any of the following: the criminal behavior was not recent, the criminal behavior was an isolated event, they were pressured or coerced to commit the crime and those pressures are no longer in the applicant's life, the person did not voluntarily commit the crime, the applicant was acquitted of the crime, or they have been successfully rehabilitated from the crime.

## SECURITY VIOLATIONS

Any applicant who has demonstrated noncompliance with security regulations raises significant concern over his or her ability to safeguard classified information. Any individual who has a history of any unauthorized disclosure of classified information, or violations of security regulations that are deliberate or multiple will be denied a security clearance. The applicants can help to mitigate concerns if they can prove that the noncompliance with security regulations were inadvertent or isolated, were due to improper or inadequate training, and that they are committed to safeguarding classified information.

## OUTSIDE ACTIVITIES

Involvement in particular employment or activities may present security concerns if it goes against the principle of the United States or if it would place the applicant in a position of increased pressure to divulge classified information. Examples of this would include any compensated employment or volunteer work with countries other than the United States, with foreign nationals, or with organizations that represent interests that may be detrimental to the United States. Any applicant who is involved in the analysis and/or discussion of, or who authors material on intelligence, defense, foreign affairs, or protected technology would be suspected of having undue external influences.

Applicants can mitigate these concerns by ceasing all activities or employment that would conflict with the United States, or by proving that no conflict exists.

## MISUSE OF INFORMATION TECHNOLOGY SYSTEMS

Any applicant who has demonstrated noncompliance with or blatant disregard for rules, procedures, or guidelines for information technology systems will pose a significant security risk to the United States. It is critical that applicants can be entrusted to take all precautions to safeguard electronic information processing, transfer, and storage.

There will be significant security concerns if an applicant has any history of illegal or unauthorized entry into any information technology system. Applicants who illegally or inappropriately modified, destroyed, manipulated, or denied access to any information technology system will also be considered a grave security risk. Applicants will not be considered for security clearance if they have illegally or inappropriately removed hardware, software, or media, or introduced hardware, software, or media into an information technology system. The Department of Homeland Security views misuse or illegal activities surrounding information technology to be a very serious threat to national security. Applicants with any history of such activities will have a difficult time proving that they will not be a security threat.

Applicants can mitigate concerns by proving any of the following: the misuse was not significant in nature, it was not recent, the conduct was unintentional or accidental, the introduction or removal of media was authorized, or that any misuse was immediately followed by rapid, good faith efforts to correct the action.

## APPEALING A DENIAL OF CLEARANCE

A potential employee who is denied clearance does not have much recourse. Many positions within the DHS require a security clearance that must be assured prior to the formal unconditional offer of employment. If the candidate is found unsuitable for any reason, he or she simply will not be extended an offer of employment with the DHS. It is much easier for the DHS to withdraw the conditional offer of employment than it will be to deal with the appeals process. A candidate can still appeal the decision; however, it most likely will be a losing battle since the conditional offer of employment will be withdrawn.

Current employees who are denied clearance can appeal the decision. Executive Order 12968, "Access to Classified Information," describes the process for federal or government civilian personnel to appeal. An appeal is filed, and heard before an administrative judge appointed by the authority authorizing the security clearance. Upon hearing all the information pertaining to the denial, the judge will render a decision. The individual who still disagrees with the decision can appeal it to the Appellate Board. The judgment rendered by this board is final and concludes the appeal process. Any candidate who is denied a security clearance will have to wait a minimum of one year before applying for another job that will require a security clearance. However, any individual who is denied a security clearance at any time will certainly face a difficult time trying to gain employment with the federal government in any job that requires a security clearance. With the abundance of job applicants, it would be far easier for the DHS to hire someone who can obtain a clearance without difficulty.

## NATURALIZED CITIZENS AND NON-UNITED STATES CITIZENS

A naturalized citizen is eligible to obtain a security clearance; however, non–United States citizens are not eligible. In the event that a non–United States citizen possesses a very unique or unusual skill that is urgently needed to support United States government operations, he or she may be issued a Limited Access Authorization (LAA). A Limited Access Authorization only allows the individual access to secret information and is revoked as soon as a United States citizen who possesses the same skills can be employed.

### QUICK FACT

Non–United States citizens are not eligible to obtain security clearance.

## TIPS FOR SPEEDING UP THE PROCESS

Prior to being asked to submit a completed SF-86, download a paper copy from the official government website at www.gsa.gov and fill it out prior to submitting the form electronically. This will allow you to be prepared to quickly and accurately fill out the form when it is requested by the DHS.

If you have consulted with a mental health professional for any reason, have the name, address, and phone number of the doctor and the facility listed in the notes section. You also will need to list all dates that you were seen.

Make sure that you list the Social Security numbers for all adults living with you. This is frequently omitted on applications, and results in significant delays.

Males born after December 31, 1959 must list their selective service number. Applicants frequently list their Social Security number in place of their selective service number. If you need your service number, call 1-847-688-6888 or visit http://www.sss.gov.

Applicants can also speed up their security clearance by taking a summer internship that requires a security clearance. It is much easier for DHS to update a current security clearance than it is to initiate the process.

Applicants should also ensure that all addresses listed for previous residences and previous employment are correct. A simple mistake such as a wrong zip code can delay the application by weeks to months as the background investigation is routed to an investigator in a different geographic location.

With many security clearances, the primary background investigator will contact you at the start of your investigation. He or she will want to make sure that your contact information they have is current and accurate, in case there are questions. The investigator will usually have some questions during the investigation, such as tracking down ex-employers who have gone out of business, or locations for businesses that have changed names or moved. The investigator will also usually let you know when he or she is going to contact your current employer so that you can let the employer know to be expecting the investigator. Out of courtesy, most investigators will wait to contact your current employer until the end of your investigation.

## WHAT WILL GENERATE A COMPREHENSIVE INVESTIGATION

- ► evidence that the subject is not a United States citizen, or has renounced or lost United States citizenship
- ► a positive response to questions pertaining to illegal drug use
- ► evidence that the applicant has dual citizenship

▶ evidence that the applicant has been employed as a consultant for a foreign government, firm, or agency

▶ evidence that the applicant has been issued a foreign passport

▶ evidence that the applicant has undergone mental health treatment with the exception of marital, family, or grief counseling with no history of violence by the applicant

▶ evidence that the applicant has been investigated for, charged with, or convicted of any criminal offense excluding minor traffic violations where the fine was less than $150

▶ evidence that the applicant has abused any alcohol or received any alcohol-related treatment

▶ evidence that the applicant has had clearance to access denied, suspended, or revoked, or if the subject has been banned from federal employment

▶ evidence that the applicant has associated with individuals or groups dedicated to the violent overthrow of the United States government

## MATERIAL THAT WILL BE REQUESTED

▶ high school transcripts (may be waived if college has been completed)

▶ college transcripts

▶ birth certificate

▶ DD-214 for those who served in the military

▶ addresses, phone numbers, and point of contact for all places of employment during the investigation period

▶ a minimum of three personal references (people whom the applicant has known for at least five years, are not family members, and were not an employer)

▶ verification and disposition of divorces, bankruptcies, or any other criminal or civil court actions

▶ criminal history records covering all locations where the applicant has lived, worked, or attended school for the last ten years

# CHAPTER thirteen

## DEVELOPING CONTACTS: THE SECRET WEAPON FOR GETTING THE JOB YOU WANT

**GETTING A** position with the DHS can be a daunting task on your own, and reaching out for help in the process is very often necessary. Developing contacts can make the task easier. You are on the path to an exciting future and you need to use every possible advantage to assist you in securing a career with the DHS.

Networking—the practice of developing contacts—can help you get your foot in the door to the career of your dreams. It consists of establishing relationships with people whose acquaintance or friendship could provide you with the opportunity to explore careers and develop your career goals, but is not necessarily a way to get a particular DHS job. It is establishing relationships where you can gather support and learn to be comfortable when asking for ideas, advice, and referrals. It is a tool to provide you with necessary information. People are an important source of knowledge, and developing contacts can help you get the inside scoop into a career field, gain valuable career information, acquire knowledge about the DHS, and make future useful business contacts. Most of all, developing contacts can help you build a federal resume that will get you noticed.

Developing contacts gives you the ability to gain a perspective about the job beyond limited information found in a job announcement. What are their daily or weekly work schedules? Do they work independently or are they teamed with a partner? These are some of the questions that only someone actually performing the job will be able to answer.

## QUICK FACT

Developing contacts in the DHS prior to applying for a position can provide you with critical information about the knowledge, skills, and abilities needed to perform the job.

Developing contacts in the DHS can also provide you with information regarding the skills, training, and abilities needed to perform the job function. It will help you identify your strengths and weaknesses. Talking with people who do the job will provide you with the details that cannot be found anywhere else. You may discover that your dream job is not what you expected. For example, if the job entailed sitting for long periods of time watching a computer monitor and that does not appeal to you, then you can rethink your career choices. However, the information learned in talking to someone in the job you're interested in can also solidify your occupational choice as being the right job for you.

Developing contacts can be as simple as striking up a conversation with contacts about their careers. Talking to people in the career of your choice can give you information as to the management styles and culture. You may prefer a regimented or military style (often referred to as a paramilitary structure) of management that dictates your activities. Several departments, agencies, and divisions within the DHS utilize this management style. Or on the flip side, you could be a person who enjoys the opportunity to be creative in your approach to your job, or likes to be outdoors, or prefers an office environment. Regardless, there is a job within the DHS just for you. Taking time to learn about the job can vastly increase your job satisfaction.

Developing contacts enables you to get referrals to potential mentors to assist you in reaching your career goals. Knowledge obtained from someone within the DHS provides you with the ability to understand the inner workings of the department, its goals, and its expectations. It can give you leads on future hirings within that specific department, agency, or division of the DHS or other openings that may be related to your interests, skills, and abilities.

## START WITH WHAT YOU KNOW

Take the time to create a list of people you already know, whether they be family members, friends, former classmates, teachers, college professors, or even local, state, or national politicians. With more than 193,000 employees in the DHS, chances are that someone you already know has an acquaintance or knows someone who can put you in touch with the right contact who can help you forward your career. Referrals from friends can provide you with a higher success rate of connecting with someone than simply cold calling. When you are referred, people tend to take more time to respond to your needs. The same holds true when developing contacts with the DHS. When discussing this with the people you already know, be specific with the type of contact you need, or the type of questions you have. By being specific, you may be directed to the best person or people who can answer your questions. Always be sure you ask their permission to use them as a reference when making the contact.

## CONTACT DHS DIRECTLY

If you do not know anyone, start with DHS directly. Contact your local DHS office, an office you are interested in, or DHS headquarters in Washington, DC. Start by asking for a human resource specialist or recruiter. The human resource specialists or recruiters may be able to refer you to personnel in the field you are interested in. Do not be disheartened if your first attempt is a failure. Remember, the person you contact may be busy and unable to talk at that time. Sometimes, the recruiter for a specific area may have other full-time non-recruiting duties assigned to him or her. For example, a special agent recruiter at a large field office may be a special agent with an active caseload who also handles recruiting duties.

Reaching out to DHS will help you understand the inner workings of the organization, ultimately making you better prepared. Ask your contact if he or she would take time to meet with you for an informational interview (more on informational interviews later in this chapter), or has time to answer a few questions. Ask when would be a good time to ask questions you have, or if the person could refer you to someone else. You may be surprised to learn that employees of the federal government do enjoy talking about their jobs. This may also provide you with the opportunity to introduce yourself to the local office. Many times, the local office has the final approval on who gets the job, and if they already know who you are, they might be looking for your application when it comes in for final selection.

### QUICK FACT

A word of caution: many of the jobs in DHS may contain Operation Security sensitive material (OPSEC) that prevents the employees from discussing certain aspects of their job.

## BE PREPARED

Before you begin the process of developing your new contacts, research the occupations in DHS that interest you to find out as much as you can about the job. Take time to make a list of what you know about the career field. Get on the Internet and research the federal government. You need to be able to understand how the government functions to understand just what DHS does. Read what is going on in the government to be up on current events. Search DHS, its history, operations, and future. Pull information from the library on DHS. Research your particular career interest. Being prepared will help you understand DHS and your career field to make you more effective in your future.

## INFORMATIONAL INTERVIEWS

An informational interview involves talking with people who are currently working in the field to get a better understanding of an occupation in which you are interested. Informal interviews also can help you develop contacts and gain valuable information you can use when filling out your federal resume.

**QUICK FACT**

Before contacting someone in the DHS with questions about a position, do everything you can to research the information yourself. The Internet is full of information and can provide you with the answers to many of your questions.

Listening is the key to an informational interview. Whether formally or informally, you can use informational interviews in your search for information. Take the time to write out specific questions defining things you want to know more about with a particular job. Always be considerate of your contact's time and use it wisely. Be prepared to meet resistance. People you contact may feel that you are calling them for a job—reassure them that you are only exploring their career field. Don't spend time asking questions you could look up yourself in this book or on the Internet.

If the opportunity presents itself, ask them if you can contact them in the future with further questions. Ask them if they are willing to look at your federal resume. They may be able to provide valuable tips to make your application get noticed. Do not be afraid to ask them if they know someone else to contact regarding the position. Developing a network of people in the DHS could very well be an important step in understanding the career field you have chosen, and assist you in getting the job you want.

## Questions to Ask in an Informational Interview

The following is a list of sample questions that you may wish to ask during your informational interviews while developing your new contacts:

▶ How did you choose this career field?
▶ What has been your career path?
▶ What was your major in college?
▶ What made you choose DHS?
▶ What do you do on a typical day?

▶ What are your major job responsibilities?

▶ What are the special requirements (i.e., training, education, certificates) for the job?

▶ What kinds of experiences are absolutely essential to the job?

▶ What is the toughest part of your job?

▶ What is the most rewarding part of your job?

▶ Describe the toughest situation you have been faced with in the job.

▶ Does the work get more interesting as you stay longer?

▶ Is there a demand for people in this field?

▶ What part of the country provides the best opportunities in this field?

▶ What is the job satisfaction in this field?

▶ What entry level positions provide the most ability to learn a great deal?

▶ What specific characteristics or personnel traits are needed for the job?

▶ What is the average length of time a person stays with the organization?

▶ What is the potential for advancement?

▶ If you were starting over again, what would you do differently?

▶ How do you see this field changing in the future?

▶ What other positions are available in the same career field?

▶ What is the most important aspect in a federal resume?

▶ What are important key words, or buzzwords, to include in the federal resume?

▶ Who do you know who might be willing to speak with me as well?

▶ How are duty positions determined, and how frequently are you required to move?

▶ Do you have to serve time overseas?

▶ May I use your name when contacting recruiters at DHS?

You probably will have other, specific questions in mind. Take the time to be prepared with questions that address what you want to know and be attentive when listening to the answers. Talking to someone will provide you with valuable information to use not only in your quest for a position with the DHS, but with other jobs you may pursue in the future. You may also discover ways you may be able to help the person in the future through the contacts that you develop in this process.

## EVALUATING INFORMATION LEARNED

Hopefully, you are able to gather new insights about the career you want utilizing an informational interview approach. Evaluate your thoughts and feelings about the occupation, workplace, and people you interviewed. Ask yourself questions like: What did I learn from the interview? What aspects of the job did I like? What aspects of the job didn't I like? Did the interview reveal any new advantages or concerns about the job? What career advice did I receive about the job? Did I discover any other occupations in the DHS that I might want to pursue? How would I fit in this type of work environment? And finally, do I think I would be happy in this type of job or organization?

Be careful that you do not allow your impressions of just one person or one visit to an organization cloud your judgment. It may have been a day when people were engaged in the "fun" tasks of the job. Or, it may have been a bad day at the office. Talk with several people in the field and confirm the information you have learned using other sources.

## SAYING THANK YOU

Taking the time to say thank you for helping demonstrates to the person that you care. It is imperative to follow up with a note or e-mail thanking your new contact for his or her assistance. Your note may be brief, just a paragraph or two expressing appreciation for the time spent. Thank the contact for the advice given, and perhaps recall a particularly helpful piece of information. Let contacts know that if you can ever be of any assistance to them, all they have to do is call. As you move toward your new career, let people know how their information proved helpful to you. A new contact you have developed may become a lifelong friend to whom you can turn with future questions or problems.

## OTHER WAYS TO NETWORK

There are other areas in which you can develop contacts in your attempt to locate more information on your career choice.

## Career Fairs

In its effort to hire the best and brightest talent, the federal government participates in local career and job fairs. A career fair is an excellent way to learn about opportunities that may be available within the DHS. The federal government has partnered with colleges and universities to provide information to make potential job candidates aware of what the federal government has to offer. Human resource specialists and recruiters who attend these job fairs provide an opportunity to ask those questions you cannot get answered reading a book or looking at a website. Bring copies of your federal resume and do not be afraid to ask them their opinion of it. Please remember when attending a job fair to be dressed in appropriate business attire. You are selling yourself at all times.

## Professional Organizations, Associations, Forums, and Blogs

Professional organizations, associations, forums, and blogs exist for just about every career and field imaginable. A simple search of the Internet utilizing words like "professional federal organizations," "federal associations," or "federal forums" will provide lists of organizations, forums, topics, and conversations covering most, if not all of the jobs found within the DHS. These professional organizations, associations, and forums serve to maintain professional standards, liaison with others in the field, and provide support. Reach out to these people with the knowledge, skills, abilities, and even the same jobs you are interested in. You can utilize their experience and skills to assist you in furthering your career with the DHS. They can provide you with a wealth of knowledge about working for a particular agency, tips to help you get the job of your dreams, or even the inside scoop about a particular job or office in the DHS.

## Seminars, Workshops, and Professional Courses

Attending government seminars, workshops, and even professional courses can put you in a position to advance your knowledge and provide you with the opportunity to introduce yourself to the leaders and other attendees. Lectures are performed by professionals in their field. For them to have achieved that status they must have developed numerous contacts themselves. Look for federal government programs found in every major city that reach out to the public. There are also state and local programs to consider. Remember, you are attempting to develop contacts. Government professionals at all levels come in contact with someone else. They may know just the person you are looking for in the DHS.

## Internships

Don't forget about the possibilities provided by internships with the DHS. An internship provides an excellent way to learn how the agency operates and gives you the opportunity to "try on" a career job position. There are both paid and unpaid intern positions available in the DHS. As an intern, you work among various departments in your field of study, effectively giving you an overview of just where you and your skills fit. A mentor provided during an internship can assist you in making critical career choices and gives you a valued contact. A large number of former interns go on in the federal government by being offered permanent positions. Specific programs also allow for noncompetitive conversion to term, career, or career-conditional appointments.

## IT'S YOUR FUTURE

Whatever your career field, developing contacts today can help you throughout your career. Learning everything that your career has to offer gives you an overview of the potential you have in shaping the future of the federal government. Having a network of contacts will give you resources that you can utilize to advance your career, and provide you with the expertise to become successful in the field. It can give you a mentor to help you throughout your career, or even have a contact within an organization to whom you can hopefully return a favor one day.

# CHAPTER fourteen

## WHAT HAPPENS IF I CHANGE MY MIND?

**FAST FORWARD** into your future. You've done your research, developed your contacts, and successfully applied for and landed that great job at the DHS. You have gotten your foot in the door, but what happens if you discover that the job you hoped for is not the job of your dreams?

First of all, don't fear, surely you have heard the term, "don't throw the baby out with the bathwater." Just because you are not happy with your present situation doesn't mean that you should give up on the DHS. The good news is so many agencies fall under the DHS umbrella that you can always look to other career possibilities within the department that may be more suited to your experience and temperament. The Bureau of Labor and Statistics indicates that people change jobs fairly often, about once every five years.[1] Most people who change occupations do so because of the prospect of better working conditions, greater status, job satisfaction, or responsibility. Since there are always opportunities to develop and change, no experience is a bad experience. The really good news is that because so many agencies fall under the DHS umbrella, you can always look to other career possibilities that may be more suited to your experience and temperament. This chapter discusses making moves within the DHS once you have started to find your best niche and to help you grow in your new career.

The federal government is full of very talented, professional, and dedicated people who work incredibly hard to make sure the nation's governmental infrastructure can function efficiently. The DHS needs more professionals to continue their mission, and can provide you with unique opportunities to challenge you mentally and physically in your job each day.

### QUICK FACT

Ninety percent of employees decide whether they will stay in an organization, or begin looking for a new job, during their first six months on the job.

The DHS is a vast organization. Sometimes new federal employees can have a negative experience at the beginning of their careers. This first impression can have a lasting effect on their view of the federal government. Your actions as an employee are especially critical during the first year as your actions will directly affect your future productivity and job satisfaction. Research conducted by the Aberdeen Group in 2006 found that 90% of employees decide whether they will stay in an organization, or begin looking for a new job, during their first six months on the job. Between 2003 and 2007 new federal employees voluntarily left their agencies at rates ranging from 10 to 18%.[2] This is an alarming rate.

New employees who received effective integration or orientation into a new job were found to be much more satisfied with their job within the first year. The orientation transition during your first year will help you focus you on the mission, vision, and culture of the organization. The Department of Homeland Security is actively taking steps to address effective integration and orientation for new employees during their first year with the federal government. If you feel that you are not matching well with your agency, you may possibly need to look elsewhere in the DHS. There are always opportunities to develop and change, and you have already learned the process of finding a job within the DHS.

Every day people enter the federal government workforce with a wide range of expectations and illusions. Some of their expectations are met, but other new employees feel left out. This disillusionment often leaves employees feeling betrayed by their employer, which in turn causes them to terminate their employment. Before you ever decide to leave the DHS, conduct research among coworkers, including asking people in the field how they make the job work for them. There has to be a reason they are still there. If you are seriously considering leaving your current agency because you are not satisfied, talk with your supervisors. Let them know how you feel. There are several programs within the federal government that can enable supervisors to assist you with job satisfaction at your current position.

The book *The 7 Hidden Reasons Employees Leave*, by Leigh Branham, lists the main reasons employees leave a job:

- ▶ the job or workplace was not as expected
- ▶ the mismatch between job and person
- ▶ too little coaching and feedback
- ▶ too few growth and advancement opportunities
- ▶ feeling devalued and unrecognized
- ▶ stress from overwork and work-life imbalance
- ▶ loss of trust and confidence in senior leaders[3]

**QUICK FACT**

Pay is frequently not one of the top reasons why people are not satisfied with their jobs.

When asked, most employers indicate that money is by far the biggest reason for employees leaving an organization. However, that is not true. The seven reasons previously listed are a more accurate representation of the reasons employees leave federal employment. This is why it is important to research your interests before you pursue a career in the DHS.


## TRANSITIONING

If you find yourself feeling frustrated, unchallenged, or unfulfilled in your job it may be time to begin a change. Ask yourself why it is that you do not like the job. Perhaps you are not challenged in the position anymore. Perhaps your interests lie with a different type of career position. It might be that you are not satisfied with a particular agency within the DHS, but would still like to work for the federal government. Give some thought to just what would make you happy and satisfied. Faced with increasing competition from the private sector for talented professionals, the federal government has taken steps to retain a hold on their investment, and you are that investment.

The Department of Homeland Security wants to keep you in the federal government and will help you locate positions that may be better suited to you. Develop a career plan for yourself. Reevaluate your goals and where you wish to succeed. Discover how you can attain those goals and dreams through your current job. Perhaps you need additional skills, or perhaps you need to change jobs to fulfill your new career plan. Whatever you decide, seek guidance from someone who can give you the insight into how the DHS can help you reach those goals.

Using the contacts you developed in the DHS, you can launch yourself into other positions in the DHS. You might be able to locate a position that is better suited to your knowledge, skills, and abilities. You may find a position that makes you feel that you contribute to the future of the agency.

## WHAT THE DHS HAS TO OFFER

Instead of focusing on the negatives of the job, take time to look at the opportunities that you can find within the DHS. Here are a few of the positive things that a career with the DHS can provide.

### Stability

You need to analyze what employment with the federal government has to offer. The first thing that may come to mind is that the federal government is thought to be a more stable employer than employment in the private sector. In today's economy, job security is highly desired but infrequently found. Layoffs in the federal government are very infrequent. Staffing reductions are generally carried out through attrition, which is simply not replacing workers who retire or leave the federal government for other reasons. This stability of employment leads to a happier lifestyle all around.

**QUICK FACT**

Layoffs in the federal government are very infrequent.

## Pay and Benefits

Pay is an important factor when stating reasons for employment with the DHS. Contrary to popular belief, the federal government pays at levels equal to the private sector. The benefit of employment with the federal government comes with federally adjusted annual cost of living allowances and locality pay, both of which increase take-home pay. A federal employee under the general schedule can receive step increases in pay for time-in-grade as well as bonuses for performance. The average annual salary for full-time workers under the general schedule in the federal government is more than $65,000. There are a wide variety of health insurance and disability options available with the federal government at a reasonable cost to you. The insurance options offered by the federal government rival any found within the largest corporations in the private sector. The federal government offers group term life insurance. There is also a three-tiered retirement plan called the Federal Employees Retirement System (FERS). The FERS plan consists of Social Security, a pension plan, and an optional thrift savings plan. The Thrift Savings Plan is the government's version of a 401(k). Most private sector companies only include a type of 401(k) program for retirement. The federal government also offers an annuity in its pension plan. Another great benefit that the federal government offers is 13 sick days a year, as well as offering 13, 20, or up to 26 days of vacation per year based on the number of years of service. Not only do you accrue many vacation days but you will also receive 10 paid holidays a year.

**QUICK FACT**

The average annual salary of full-time workers in the federal government is more than $65,000.

## Service to Your Country

When people think of serving their country, most think of the military. Working for the federal government is much more. You can perform a valuable service to the United States in the effort to protect the country from terrorism, secure our borders, and lead rescue efforts in natural and man-made disasters. Your contribution as an employee with the federal government can help shape the future.

## Opportunity for Advancement

The federal government can give you opportunities to advance throughout your career. The process starts with your basic agency training and continues throughout the life of your career. Training increases your scientific, professional, technical, and future management skills. The federal government recognizes that training and development is essential for improving the performance of an employee. Functional training helps you grow in your future advancement and leadership possibilities. The DHS will provide you with necessary skills needed to grow in an effort to retain you throughout your career. You can use this training to assist you in further advancement or new career possibilities. You also have a greater opportunity in the DHS for advancement than in the private sector. Once in the federal system, you receive priority over others applying from outside the federal government. The competitive edge will give you the opportunity to change jobs or even careers within the DHS. We discussed in an earlier chapter the fact that the federal government is offering tuition reimbursement. The federal government offers up to $10,000 per year in an effort to help pay off student loans and some DHS agencies offer tuition assistance to help you pursue a graduate degree.

## Travel

Employment with the DHS can give you challenging assignments offering you the opportunity for growth. The majority of DHS positions are located outside of Washington, DC. You could find yourself working in almost any location in the United States, or even anywhere in the world. If you like the desert, DHS is there. You may like living by the ocean, DHS is there as well. How about living in Alaska, or even Hawaii? Have you always wanted to live in a foreign land? There are positions within the DHS located globally, providing you with real possibilities for travel that you should explore.

The positive things about the DHS that have been listed here are just the personal benefits. When you work for the federal government you are giving of yourself for others. You are an important part of the function of the government of the United States.

## Midlife Career Change

There is no company in the private sector that can provide you with the opportunity to change your career as easily as you can do within the DHS. If you are a seasoned professional with years of experience you can use your knowledge, skills, and abilities to begin a new chapter in your life. Perhaps you are looking for new challenges, or even the possibility of living in a new area. You start by looking at what you have learned about the DHS and its jobs throughout your career. You will begin to see where the training and experiences gained can lead you to something totally new. Having worked with the DHS, you have hopefully developed contacts with others who can give you the insight on particular careers within the agency that interest you.

As an employee with the federal government you should continually update your federal resume to reflect your abilities. With the federal preference offered to employees of the federal government, you can apply to any and all jobs that meet your qualifications when the need arises. The really good news is many agencies fall under the DHS umbrella, and you can always look to other career possibilities that may be more suited to your experience and temperament.

## IF YOU CHANGE JOBS

So you find a new job. What should you do now? Moving from your old job to your new job should be conducted with grace. You never want to alienate those you leave behind. You never know, but your previous employer may be contacted in the future for a recommendation on your updated security clearance. Someone you may have worked with previously may come to work in your new office in the future. Be sure you provide your old supervisor adequate notice. Two weeks is the industry standard. If you need more time than two weeks, negotiate delaying the start of your new job with your new boss. Your new employer will recognize that you are trying to be courteous to your old employer, and will usually work with you. When leaving, always emphasize the positive. Make the fact known that leaving was a difficult decision. Explain why you are drawn to the new position. Help smooth the transition—let your old boss know you can finish a project or help train your replacement.

Make sure you complete all the necessary checkout procedures for the office and agency. Remember to stay in touch with your former coworkers after you leave. Make an effort to call or write them. They are still an important contact that you may be able to utilize in the future.

## WHATEVER YOU DECIDE

Whatever you decide to do, remember you have worked hard to secure a future with the Department of Homeland Security, an organization that is on the cutting edge. With the vital responsibilities found throughout the DHS you can be confident that you have a significant part in shaping the future of the United States government. Be proud of your accomplishment.

# Appendix A

## Colleges and Universities That Offer Certificates or Degrees in Homeland Security

At the time of publication there are almost 300 different programs in homeland security that are offered at colleges and universities in the United States. These programs include certifications, associate degrees, bachelor degrees, master degrees, post-master certifications, and doctoral degrees. These programs are being offered in the traditional brick and mortar setting as well as online using a distance-learning format.

More colleges and universities will be introducing new Homeland Security programs starting in the fall of 2010 and the spring of 2011. The Department of Homeland Security currently maintains a list of Homeland Security programs offered in the United States at www.dhs.gov. If you do not see the school of your choice, you should contact the enrollment office of the school to see if they will be offering a program in Homeland Security.

*Listed alphabetically by state then by college or university*

**Alabama**

No programs currently available.

**Alaska**

No programs currently available.

**Arizona**

Arizona State University

Phoenix, AZ

Bachelor's in Applied Studies in
Emergency Management

www.asu.edu

Embry Riddle Aeronautical
University at Prescott

Prescott, AZ

Bachelor of Science in Global
Security and Intelligence Studies

www.erau.edu

Everest Online

Phoenix, AZ

Associate of Science in Homeland
Security

Bachelor of Science in Homeland
Security

http://www.everestonline.edu

Grand Canyon University

Phoenix, AZ

Bachelor of Science in Emergency
Management

Bachelor of Science in Public Safety
Administration

Emergency Management
Certificate—Health Care

Emergency Management
Certificate—Public Safety

Master of Science in Executive Fire
Service Leadership

Master of Science in Leadership
with an emphasis in Disaster
Preparedness and Crisis
Management

www.my.gcu.edu

Northcentral University

Prescott Valley, AZ

Doctor of Philosophy in Business
Administration with Homeland
Security Specialization

Master of Business Administration
with Homeland Security
Specialization

www.ncu.edu

**Arkansas**

Arkansas Tech University

Russellville, AR

Master of Science Degree in
Emergency Management and
Homeland Security

Bachelor of Science in Emergency
Administration & Management

www.atu.edu

**California**

California State University

Long Beach, CA

Master of Science in Emergency
Service Administration

www.csulb.edu

Casa Loma College
Hawthorne, CA
Emergency Management Studies
www.casalomacollege.edu

Henley-Putnam University
San Jose, CA
Bachelor of Science in Intelligence
    Management
Bachelor of Science in Terrorism
    and Counterterrorism Studies
Bachelor of Science in Management
    of Personal Protection
Master of Science in Intelligence
    Management
Master of Science in Terrorism and
    Counterterrorism Studies
Master of Science in Management
    of Personal Protection
Doctorate of Strategic Security
www.henley-putnam.edu

Loma Linda University
Loma Linda, CA
Post Bachelor of Science Certificate in
    Emergency Preparedness and
    Response
www.llu.edu

National University
La Jolla, CA
Master of Science in Homeland
    Security and Safety Engineering
www.nu.edu

Naval Postgraduate School
Monterey, CA
Homeland Security Master of Arts
    Program
www.chds.us

San Diego State University
San Diego, CA
Master of Science in Public Health—
    Specialization in Global Emergency
    Preparedness and Response
Interdisciplinary Master's Degree in
    Homeland Security
www.sdsu.edu

Touro University International
Cypress, CA
Graduate Certificate in Emergency
    Management
www.tuiu.edu

University of Southern California
Los Angeles, CA
Master of Science in System Safety
    and Security
Graduate Certificate in System
    Safety and Security
www.usc.edu

**Colorado**
Colorado Technical University
Colorado Springs, CO
Master of Science in Management with a
    concentration in Homeland Security
Doctor of Management with a
    concentration in Homeland Security
www.coloradotech.edu

Community College of Denver
Denver, CO
Public Security Management
    Certificate Program
www.ccd.edu

Pikes Peak Community College
Colorado Springs, CO
Homeland Security/Emergency
    Management Associate of
    Applied Science Degree and
    Certificate Programs
www2.ppcc.edu

Red Rocks Community College
Lakewood, CO
Associate of Applied Science in
    Emergency Management &
    Planning
Associate of Applied Science
    Certificate in Emergency
    Management & Planning
www.rrcc.edu

University of Colorado—Colorado
    Springs
Colorado Springs, CO
Undergraduate Certificate in
    Homeland Security
Graduate Certificate in Homeland
    Defense
Undergraduate Certificate in
    Disaster Public Health
Graduate Certificate in Disaster
    Public Health

Bachelor of Arts in Criminal Justice
    with an emphasis in Homeland
    Security
Master of Public Administration with
    an emphasis in Homeland
    Security
www.uccs.edu

University of Denver
Denver, CO
Master of Arts in Homeland Security
www.du.edu

**Connecticut**
Capital Community College
Hartford, CT
Emergency Management Response
    Certificate
www.ccc.edu

Goodwin College
East Hartford, CT
Associate Degree in Science in
    Homeland Security
www.goodwincollege.edu

University of Connecticut
Storrs, CT
Online Master of Professional
    Studies Degree in Homeland
    Security Leadership
www.uconn.edu

University of New Haven
New Haven, CT
Graduate Certificate in National
   Security
www.newhaven.edu

## Delaware

Wilmington College
New Castle, DE
Master of Science Administration of
   Justice with a concentration in
   Homeland Security
Post Master's Certificate in Homeland
   Security
www.wilmu.edu

## District of Columbia

Georgetown University
Washington, DC
Graduate Certificate in Biodefense and
   Public Safety
Certificate in Homeland Security
www.georgetown.edu

The George Washington University
Washington, DC
Doctor of Science: Engineering
   Management and Systems
   Engineering with a concentration in
   Crisis, Emergency, and Risk
   Management
Master of Science: Engineering
   Management with a concentration in
   Crisis, Emergency, and Risk
   Management

Graduate Certificate in Homeland
   Security Emergency Preparedness
   and Response
Graduate Certificate in Emergency
   Management and Public Health
www.gwu.edu

## Florida

Embry-Riddle Aeronautical University
Daytona Beach, FL
Bachelor of Science in Homeland
   Security (Daytona campus)
Certificate in Security and Intelligence
   (Worldwide campus)
www.erau.edu

Everest College, Pompano Beach
Pompano Beach, FL
Associate of Science in Homeland
   Security
Bachelor of Science in Homeland
   Security
www.everest.edu

Jacksonville State University
Jacksonville, FL
Master of Public Administration in
   Emergency Management
Master of Science in Emergency
   Management
Graduate Certificate in Emergency
   Management
Bachelor of Science Minor in Homeland
   Security
www.jsu.edu

Kaplan College (Online)
Ft. Lauderdale, FL
Terrorism and National Security
    Management Certificate
www.cj.kaplan.edu

Keiser University
Ft. Lauderdale, FL
Associate of Arts Degree in Homeland
    Security
Bachelor of Arts Degree in Homeland
    Security
www.keiseruniversity.edu

Lynn University
Boca Raton, FL
Minor and Certificate Program in
    Emergency and Disaster
    Management
Master of Science and Certificate
    Program in Administration
    Emergency Planning and
    Administration
www.lynn.edu

Northwest Florida State College
Niceville, FL
Associate of Applied Science in
    Emergency Administration
    Management
www.owcc.cc.fl.us

St. Petersburg College
St. Petersburg, FL
Certificate in Homeland Security
Associate of Science Degree in
    Criminal Justice Technology with a
    concentration in Homeland Security
Certificate in Emergency Administration
    and Management
Associate of Science in Emergency
    Administration and Management
www.spcollege.edu

University of Central Florida
Orlando, FL
Minor in Emergency Management and
    Homeland Security
www.ucf.edu

University of Southern Florida
Tampa, FL
Graduate Certificate in Homeland
    Security
www.usf.edu

**Georgia**
Central Georgia Technical College
Macon, GA
Associate's Degree in Emergency
    Management
www.cgtcollege.org

Chattahoochee Technical College
Marietta, GA
Associate's Degree in Fire Science
Associate of Applied Science in
    Homeland Security
Associate Degree in Emergency
    Management
www.chattcollege.com

Georgia State University
Atlanta, GA
Graduate Certificate in Disaster
    Management
www.gsu.edu

Gwinnett Technical College
Lawrenceville, GA
Emergency Services Education
    Programs
www.gwinnetttechnicalcollege.com

## Hawaii
Chaminade University of Honolulu
Honolulu, HI
Homeland Security Master of Criminal
    Justice Administration Track
www.chaminade.edu

University of Hawaii—West O'ahu
Pearl City, HI
Certificate in Disaster Preparedness
    and Emergency Management
www.uhwo.hawaii.edu

## Idaho
Canyon College
Caldwell, ID
Bachelor of Arts in Homeland Security
www.canyoncolleg.edu

## Illinois
Adler School of Professional
    Psychology
Chicago, IL
Master of Arts in Police Psychology
www.adler.edu

Benedictine University
Lisle, IL
Master's in Public Health with a
    Concentration in Disaster
    Management
Certificate in Disaster Management
www.ben.edu

College of Lake County
Grayslake, IL
Certificate in Emergency and Disaster
    Management
www.clcillinois.edu

Frontier Community College
Fairfield, IL
Associate's Degree in Emergency
    Preparedness & Emergency
    Disaster Services
Certificate in Emergency Preparedness
    & Emergency Disaster Services
www.iecc.edu

University of Illinois at Chicago
Chicago, IL
Certificate in Emergency Management
    and Continuity Planning
www.uic.edu

### Indiana

Indiana University—Kokomo
Kokomo, IN
Certificate in Homeland
    Security/Emergency Management
www.iuk.edu

Indiana University—Purdue
    University Fort Wayne
Fort Wayne, IN
Certificate in Risk and Emergency
    Management
www.ipfw.edu

Purdue University, Homeland
    Security Institute
West Lafayette, IN
Graduate-Level Area of Specialization
    in Homeland Security
www.purdue.edu

Vincennes University
Vincennes, IN
Bachelor of Science in Homeland
    Security and Public Safety
www.vinu.edu

### Iowa

Iowa Central Community College
    Homeland Security Training Center
Fort Dodge, IA
Basic Homeland Security Training
www.iowacentral.edu

Upper Iowa University
Fayette, IA
Master of Public Administration with
    Homeland Security Emphasis
Bachelor of Science in Emergency and
    Disaster Management
www.manchester.uiu.edu

Western Iowa Tech Community
    College
Sioux City, IA
Associate of Applied Science in
    Emergency and Disaster
    Management
www.witcc.com

### Kansas

Barton County Community College
Great Bend, KS
Associate in Applied Science,
    Hazardous Materials Environmental
    Compliance
Certificate in Hazardous Materials
www.barton.cc.ks.us

Hesston College
Hesston, KS
Associate in Arts Degree in Disaster
    Management
www.hesston.edu

Southwestern College
Wichita, KS
Bachelor of Science Degree in Security
    Management
Certificate in Homeland Security
Master of Science in Security
    Administration
www.southwesterncollege.org

**Kentucky**

Eastern Kentucky University Justice
    and Safety Center
Richmond, KY
Bachelor of Science in Homeland
    Security
Master of Science in Safety, Security
    and Emergency Management
www.eku.edu

**Louisiana**

Baton Rouge Community College
Baton Rouge, LA
Certificate in Emergency Management
www.mybrcc.edu

Delgado Community College
New Orleans, LA
Certificate of Technical Studies in
    Homeland Security and Emergency
    Management
www.dcc.edu

Louisiana State University
Baton Rouge, LA
Master of Science (or Arts) with a Minor
    in Disaster Science and
    Management
Bachelor of Science—Minor in Disaster
    Science and Management
www.lsu.edu

Tulane University
New Orleans, LA
Bachelor of Arts in Security Studies—
    Minor in Homeland Security Studies
Post-Baccalaureate Certificate in
    Homeland Security Studies
www.tulane.edu

**Maine**

No programs currently available.

**Maryland**

Anne Arundel Community College
Arnold, MD
Associate of Applied Science in
    Homeland Security Management
www.aacc.edu

Frederick Community College
Frederick, MD
Associate of Applied Science in
    Emergency Management
www.frederick.edu

Johns Hopkins University
Baltimore, MD
Master of Arts in Government with a
    concentration in Securities Studies
Certificate in National Security
www.jhu.edu

National Consortium for the Study of
    Terrorism and Responses to
    Terrorism
College Park, MD
Graduate Fellowship Program
Undergraduate Research Program
www.start.umd.edu

Towson University
Towson, MD
Master of Science in Homeland
    Security Management
Post-Baccalaureate Certificate in
    Security Assessment and
    Management
www.towson.edu

University of Maryland—University
    College
Adelphi, MD
Bachelor of Science in Homeland
    Security
Minor in Terrorism Studies

Homeland Security Management
    Graduate Certificate
Security Management Undergraduate
    Certificate
Bio-Security Undergraduate Certificate
Bachelor of Science in Emergency
    Management
www.umuc.edu

## Massachusetts

Anna Maria College
Paxton, MA
Master of Science in Emergency
    Management
Certificate in Emergency Management
www.annamaria.edu

Curry College
Certificate in Homeland Defense
www.curry.edu

Massachusetts Maritime Academy
Buzzards Bay, MA
Bachelor of Science in Emergency
    Management
Master of Science in Emergency
    Management
www.maritime.edu

National Graduate School (Online)
Master of Science in Homeland
    Security
Homeland Security Certificate
www.ngs.edu

UMassOnline (University of
Massachusetts)
Bachelor of Science in Emergency
Management
Certificate Program in Security
Management and Homeland
Security
www.umassonline.net

University of Massachusetts—Lowell
Lowell, MA
Certificate Program in Security
Management and Homeland
Security
Graduate Certificate in Security Studies
www.uml.edu

## Michigan

Michigan State University
East Lansing, MI
Certificate in Homeland Security
Studies
Online Certificate in Homeland Security
Studies
www.msu.edu

Siena Heights University
Adrian, MI
Master of Arts in Homeland Security
Master of Arts in Emergency
Management
Master of Arts in Nuclear Power
www.sienaheight.edu

St. Clair County Community College
Port Huron, MI
Understanding and Combating
Terrorism Certificate
Investigating, Preventing & Surviving
Terrorism Certificate (police officers
only)
Preventing, Identifying and Investigating
Terrorism Certificate
www.sc4.edu

## Minnesota

Cappella University
Minneapolis, MN
Bachelor of Science in Public Safety
with Homeland Security or
Emergency Management
Specialization
Master of Science in Public Safety with
Emergency Management
Specialization
Doctor of Philosophy in Public Safety
with Emergency Management
Specialization
www.capella.edu

Hennepin Technical College
Brooklyn Park, MN
Emergency Medical Services Specialist
Certificate
Advanced Technical Certificate in
Emergency Management
www.hennepintech.edu

Minneapolis Community & Technical
College
Minneapolis, MN
Associate of Applied Science in
Homeland Security
Certificate in Homeland Security or
Homeland Security Planning
Certificate in Homeland Security
Emergency Management
www.minneapolis.edu

## Mississippi

Meridian Community College
Meridian, MS
Associate of Applied Science in Fire
Protection Technology
Associate of Applied Science in
Emergency Management
Associate of Applied Science in
Communications Technology
www.mcc.cc.ms.us

## Missouri

Grantham University
Kansas City, MO
Online Bachelor of Science Degree in
Criminal Justice with Homeland
Security Specialty
www.grantham.edu

Park University
Parkville, MO
Master in Public Administration with a
concentration in Disaster &
Emergency Management
Certificate in Public Administration,
Disaster and Emergency
Management
www.park.edu

University of Central Missouri
Warrensburg, MO
Bachelor of Science in Crisis and
Disaster Management
www.ucmo.edu

University of Missouri Extension,
Columbia
Columbia, MO
Certificate in Community Emergency
Management
www.missouri.edu

Webster University
St. Louis, MO
Master of Arts in Business and
Organizational Security
Management
www.webster.edu

## Montana

No programs currently available.

## Nebraska

No programs currently available.

## Nevada

College of Southern Nevada

Las Vegas, NV

Associate of Arts in Emergency
Management Administration

www.csn.edu

University of Nevada—Las Vegas

Las Vegas, NV

Master of Science in Crisis and
Emergency Management

Certificate in Homeland Defense and
Security

www.unlv.edu

## New Hampshire

Daniel Webster College

Nashua, NH

Bachelor of Science in Homeland
Security

www.dwc.edu

Rivier College

Nashau, NH

Online Certificate in Homeland Security

Online Certificate in Emergency and
Disaster Management

www.rivier.edu

## New Jersey

Cumberland County Community
College

Vineland, NJ

Homeland Security Certificate

www.cccnj.net

Fairleigh Dickinson University

Madison, NJ

Undergraduate Security & Terrorism
Studies Certificate

Graduate Certificate in Global Security
and Terrorism Studies

Master of Science in Homeland
Security

www.fdu.edu

New Jersey City University

Jersey City, NJ

Master of Science in Professional
Securities Studies

Executive Doctor of Professional
Studies in Professional Security
Leadership, Management and Policy

Bachelor of Science in Professional
Security Studies

www.njcu.edu

New Jersey Institute of Technology

Newark, NJ

Graduate Certificate in Emergency
Management

Graduate Certificate in Network
Security and Information Assurance

www.njit.edu

The Richard Stockton College of
New Jersey

Pomona, NJ

Master of Arts in Criminal Justice:
Homeland Security Track

www.stockton.edu

Thomas Edison State College

Trenton, NJ

Bachelor of Science in Health Science
in Emergency Disaster Services

Associate of Science in Public and
Social Services in Emergency
Disaster Services

Graduate Certificate in Homeland
Security

www.tesc.edu

### New Mexico

No programs currently available.

### New York

Adelphi University

Garden City, NY

Graduate Certificate in Emergency
Management

www.adelphi.edu

Erie Community College—South
Campus

Orchard Park, NY

Associate of Applied Science in
Emergency Management

www.ecc.edu

Excelsior College

Albany, NY

Bachelor of Science in Criminal Justice
with Homeland Security Emphasis

Homeland Security Certificate

www.excelsior.edu

John Jay College of Criminal Justice

New York, NY

Bachelor of Arts in Fire and Emergency
Service

Certificate in Security Management
Studies

Master of Arts Certificate in Terrorism
Studies

www.jjay.cuny.edu

Long Island University

Brookville, NY

Master of Science in Homeland
Security Management (online)

Graduate-Level Advanced Certificate in
Homeland Security Management
(online)

www.southhampton.liu.edu

Long Island University—Riverhead

Riverhead, NY

Master of Science in Homeland
Security Management

Certificate in Homeland Security
Management

www.southhampton.liu.edu

Metropolitan College of New York

New York, NY

Master in Public Administration in
Emergency and Disaster
Management

www.metropolitan.edu

New York University

New York, NY

Graduate Certificate in Enterprise Risk
    Management

www.nyu.edu

Niagara County Community College

Sanborn, NY

Associate of Applied Science in
    Emergency Management

www.niagaracc.suny.edu

Onondaga Community College

Syracuse, NY

Associate of Applied Science in
    Emergency Management

www.sunyocc.edu

Pace University

New York, NY

Master of Arts in Management for
    Public Safety and Homeland
    Security Professionals

www.pace.edu

Rochester Institute of Technology

Rochester, NY

Master of Science in Cross Disciplinary
    Professional Studies with
    concentrations in Counterterrorism,
    Weapons of Mass Destruction
    Threat Assessment and Defense,
    and Cybersecurity

Certificate in Disaster & Emergency
    Management

www.rit.edu

State University of New York—
    Canton College of Technology

Canton, NY

Bachelor of Technology in Emergency
    Management

www.canton.edu

State University of New York—
    Empire State College

Saratoga Springs, NY

Bachelor of Science in Emergency
    Management

Bachelor of Science in Fire Services
    Administration

Bachelor of Science in Homeland
    Security

Bachelor of Professional Studies in
    Emergency Management

Bachelor of Professional Studies in Fire
    Services Administration

Bachelor of Professional Studies in
    Homeland Security

www.esc.edu

State University of New York—Ulster

Ulster, NY

Associate in Applied Science in
    Emergency Management

www.sunyulster.edu

Syracuse University

Syracuse, NY

Graduate Certificate in National
    Security and Counterterrorism Law

Graduate Certificate in Security Studies

www.syr.edu

## North Carolina

Caldwell Community College and
    Technical Institute
Hudson, NC
Associate of Science in Emergency
    Preparedness Technology
Certificate with Emergency
    Management Concentration
www.cccti.edu

Durham Technical Community
    College
Durham, NC
Associate of Science in Emergency
    Preparedness Technology
www.durhamtech.edu

East Carolina University
Greenville, NC
Undergraduate Minor in Security
    Studies
Online Graduate Certificate in Security
    Studies
www.ecu.edu

Nash Community College
Rocky Mount, NC
Associate of Science in Emergency
    Preparedness Technology
www.nashcc.edu

University of North Carolina—
    Chapel Hill
Chapel Hill, NC
Certificate in Community Preparedness
    and Disaster Management
www.unc.edu

Western Carolina University
Cullowhee, NC
Bachelor of Science in Emergency
    Management
www.wcu.edu

## North Dakota

North Dakota State University—
    Fargo, ND
Master of Arts in Emergency
    Management and Criminal Justice
www.ndsu.edu

## Ohio

Columbus State Community College
Columbus, OH
Associate's Degrees in Emergency
    Medical Services and Fire Science
www.cscc.edu

Lakeland Community College
Kirtland, OH
Associate Degree in Emergency
    Management Planning and
    Administration
Certificate in Emergency Management
    Planning and Administration
www.lakelandcc.edu

Notre Dame College
South Euclid, OH
Certificate in Intelligence Analysis
Bachelor of Science in Intelligence
    Analysis
www.notredamecollege.edu

Ohio Dominican University
Columbus, OH
Certificate in Homeland Security
www.ohiodominican.edu

Ohio State University
Columbus, OH
International Studies Major with
    Security and Intelligence
    Specialization with a Minor in
    Security and Intelligence
www.osu.edu

Owens Community College
Toledo, OH
Associate of Applied Science Degree—
    School of Public Safety and
    Emergency Preparedness
www.owens.edu

Tiffin University
Tiffin, OH
Bachelor of Science in Criminal Justice
    with a Homeland Security Major
www.tiffin.edu

University of Akron
Akron, OH
Bachelor of Science in Emergency
    Management with a Minor in Politics
    of Homeland Security
Certificate Degree in Emergency
    Management
www.uakron.edu

University of Cincinnati/Clermont
    College
Cincinnati, OH
Certificate in Homeland Security
www.polisci.uc.edu

University of Findlay
Findlay, OH
Masters in Environmental, Safety and
    Health Management
Bachelor of Science in Environmental,
    Safety and Occupation Health
    Management
Graduate Certificate in Emergency
    Management and Safety and Health
    Management
Terrorism Preparedness Training
    Courses
www.findlay.edu

### Oklahoma

Oklahoma State University—Oklahoma City

Oklahoma City, OK

Bachelor of Science in Technology in Emergency Responder Administration

Associate's in Applied Science in Emergency Management

www.osuokc.edu

University of Oklahoma Health Sciences Center

Norman, OK

Master's in Public Health in Public Health Preparedness and Terrorism Response

www.ouhsc.edu

University of Tulsa

Tulsa, OK

Information Security Certificate Program

www.utulsa.edu

### Oregon

Clackamas Community College

Oregon City, OR

Associate's in Applied Science in Emergency Management

www.clackamas.edu

Portland Community College

Portland, OR

Associate's in Applied Science in Fire Protection Technology

www.pcc.edu

### Pennsylvania

Bucks County Community College

Newtown, PA

Associate's in Emergency Management and Public Safety

Certificate in Emergency Management and Public Safety

www.bucks.edu

California University of Pennsylvania

California, PA

Master's in Legal Studies: Homeland Security

Certificate in Homeland Security

www.cup.edu

Central Pennsylvania College

Summerdale, PA

Bachelor of Science in Information Technology with Cyber Security Minor

www.centralpenn.edu

Delaware County Community College

Philadelphia, PA

Emergency Management and Planning, Associate in Applied Science

www.dccc.edu

Indiana University of Pennsylvania
Indiana, PA
Master of Science in Science for
    Disaster Response
Bachelor of Science Degree in Science
    of Disaster Response
www.iup.edu

Mercyhurst College, Institute for
    Intelligence Studies
Erie, PA
Online certificate in Intelligence Studies
www.mercyhurst.edu

Millersville University: Center for
    Disaster Research & Education
Millersville, PA
Master of Science Degree in
    Emergency Management
www.millersville.edu

Montgomery County Community
    College
Pottstown, PA
Associate's in Applied Science in
    Emergency Management and
    Planning
Certification in Emergency
    Management and Planning
www.mc3.edu

Penn State Hershey College of
    Medicine
Hershey, PA
Master of Homeland Security in Public
    Health Preparedness
www.psu.edu

Penn State University
University Park, PA
Certificate in Homeland Security and
    Defense
Master of Homeland Security in Public
    Health Preparedness
Graduate Certificate in Bioterrorism
    Preparedness
www.psu.edu

Penn State University, Fayette's
    Center for Community and Public
    Safety
Uniontown, PA
Non-Credit Certificate in Homeland
    Security
www.psu.edu

Philadelphia University
Philadelphia, PA
Master of Science Disaster Medicine
    and Management
www.philau.edu

Saint Joseph's University

Philadelphia, PA

Master of Science in Public Safety
Management

Master of Science in Public Safety
Management with a concentration in
Law Enforcement Administration

Master of Science in Environmental
Protection and Safety Management

Post Bachelor's and Post Master's
Certificate in Public Safety and
Environmental Protection, and
Safety Management

www.sju.edu

**Rhode Island**

Salve Regina University

Newport, RI

Master of Science in Administration of
Justice with a concentration in
Justice and Homeland Security

Certificate of Graduate Studies in
Homeland Security

www.salve.edu

**South Carolina**

No programs currently available.

**South Dakota**

No programs currently available.

**Tennessee**

Austin Peay State University

Clarksville, TN

Bachelor of Science in Criminal Justice
with a Homeland Security
Concentration

www.apsu.edu

Southwest Tennessee Community
College

Memphis, TN

Technical Certificate of Credit for
Homeland Security

www.southwest.tn.edu

University of Tennessee—Knoxville

Knoxville, TN

Homeland Security Concentration for
PhD in Nursing and Master of
Science in Nursing

Interdisciplinary Certificate in
Homeland Security Studies
(non-nurses)

www.utk.edu

**Texas**

Lamar Institute of Technology

Beaumont, TX

Associate of Applied Science in
Homeland Security

Certificate of Completion in Homeland
Security

Six Certificates in Homeland Security

www.lit.edu

San Antonio College
San Antonio, TX
Associate of Science in Emergency
  Management
www.accd.edu

Texas A&M University
College Station, TX
Online Graduate Certificate in
  Homeland Security
Master's Degree Program in Homeland
  Security
www.tamu.edu

University of North Texas
Denton, TX
Bachelor of Science in Emergency
  Administration and Planning
www.unt.edu

West Texas A&M University
Canyon, TX
Bachelor of Science in Emergency
  Management Administration
www.wtamu.edu

## Utah

University of Utah—The Rocky
  Mountain Center
Salt Lake City, UT
Certificate in Safety. Short Courses,
  Non-Degreed
www.rocky.utah.edu

Utah Valley University
Orem, UT
Bachelor of Science in Public
  Emergency Services Management
www.uvsc.edu

## Vermont

Norwich University
Northfield, VT
Master of Science in Business
  Continuity Management
www.norwich.edu

## Virginia

George Mason University
Fairfax, VA
Doctor of Philosophy in Biodefense
Master of Public Administration with a
  concentration in Emergency
  Management and Homeland
  Security
Master of Science in Biodefense
Graduate Certificate in Emergency
  Management and Homeland
  Security
www.gmu.edu

Northern Virginia Community
  College—Manassas Campus
Manassas, VA
Associate's in Applied Science
  Emergency Medical Services
www.nvcc.edu

Tidewater Community College
Norfolk, VA
Associate's in Applied Science Degree
in Technical Studies: Homeland
Security with Homeland Security
and Emergency Management Tracks
www.tcc.edu

University of Richmond (VA)
Richmond, VA
Master of Disaster Science
Bachelor of Applied Studies with Minors
in Emergency Management,
Business Continuity, Homeland
Defense
Associate's in Applied Science in
Emergency Management
Undergraduate and Post-Baccalaureate
Certificates in Emergency
Management, Business Continuity
or Homeland Defense
www.richmond.edu

Virginia Commonwealth University
Richmond, VA
Bachelor of Arts in Homeland Security
and Emergency Preparedness
Graduate Certificate in Homeland
Security and Emergency
Preparedness
Master of Arts in Homeland Security
and Emergency Preparedness
www.vcu.edu

## Washington

University of Washington
Seattle, WA
Master's in Strategic Planning for
Critical Infrastructures—Leadership
Program for Homeland Security
www.washington.edu

## West Virginia

American Military University
Charles Town, WV
Bachelor of Arts in Emergency and
Disaster Management
Master of Arts in Emergency and
Disaster Management
Bachelor of Arts in Homeland Security
Master of Arts in Homeland Security
www.amu.edu

American Public University
Charles Town, WV
Master of Arts in Homeland Security
Bachelor of Arts in Homeland Security
Bachelor of Arts in Emergency and
Disaster Management
Master of Arts in Emergency and
Disaster Management
www.apu.edu

Fairmont State Community and
Technical College
Fairmont, WV
Associate's in Applied Science Degree
in Homeland Security
www.fairmontstate.edu

Mountain State University

Beckley, WV

Bachelor of Science Degree in Criminal
Justice with Homeland Security
Concentration

www.mountainstate.edu

New River Community & Technical
College

Beckley, WV

Associate's in Applied Science in
Emergency Management

www.newriver.edu

Pierpont Community & Technical
College of Fairmont State
University

Fairmont, WV

Associate of Science in Homeland
Security

www.fairmontstate.edu

## Wisconsin

Lakeshore Technical College

Cleveland, WI

Associate's in Applied Science in
Emergency Management

www.gotoltc.com

Marian University

Fond du Lac, WI

Homeland Security Leadership
Certificate

Bachelor of Science in Homeland
Security and Minor in Homeland
Security

www.marionuniversity.edu

## Wyoming

Casper Community College

Casper, WY

Associate's in Applied Science in
Emergency Management

www.caspercollege.edu

Laramie County Community College

Cheyenne, WY

Associate of Science Degree in
Homeland Security

Certificate in Homeland Security

www.lccc.wy.edu

# Appendix B

# Colleges and Universities That Offer Four-Year Bachelor's Degrees in Criminal Justice and Law Enforcement

*Listed alphabetically by state and then by college or university*

### Alabama

Columbia Southern University
Orange Beach, AL
www.columbiasouthern.edu

Judson College
Marion, AL
www.judson.edu

Samford University
Birmingham, AL
www.samford.edu

Virginia College at Huntsville
Huntsville, AL
www.vc.edu

### Alaska

*None that offer BA degrees*

### Arizona

Arizona State University West
Phoenix, AZ
www.west.asu.edu

Northcentral University
Prescott Valley, AZ
www.ncu.edu

Northern Arizona University
Flagstaff, AZ
www.nau.edu

University of Arizona
Tucson, AZ
www.arizona.edu

University of Phoenix
Phoenix, AZ
www.phoenix.edu

**Arkansas**
University of Arkansas, Fort Smith
Fort Smith, AR
www.uafortsmith.edu

**California**
California Baptist University
Riverside, CA
www.calbaptist.edu

California State University
www.calstate.edu

> Dominguez Hills Campus
> Carson, CA
> www.csudh.edu
>
> East Bay Campus
> Hayward, CA
> www.csueastbay.edu
>
> Los Angeles Campus
> Los Angeles, CA
> www.calstatela.edu
>
> San Bernardino Campus
> San Bernardino, CA
> www.csusb.edu

National University
San Diego, CA
www.nu.edu

San Diego State University
San Diego, CA
www.sdsu.edu

Sonoma State University
Rohnert Park, CA
www.sonoma.edu

Westwood College of Technology
Los Angeles, CA
www.westwood.edu

**Colorado**
Johnson & Wales University
Denver, CO
www.jwu.edu

Metropolitan State College of
Denver
Denver, CO
www.mscd.edu

University of Colorado, Colorado
Springs
Colorado Springs, CO
www.uccs.edu

Westwood College of Technology,
Denver South
Denver, CO
www.westwood.edu

**Connecticut**
Sacred Heart University
Fairfield, CT
www.sacredheart.edu

University of New Haven
West Haven, CT
www.newhaven.edu

# Bachelor's Degrees in Criminal Justice and Law Enforcement

## Delaware

*None that offer BA degrees*

## District of Columbia

Trinity Washington University

Washington, DC

www.trinitydc.edu

## Florida

Bethune-Cookman University

Daytona Beach, CA

www.cookman.edu

Edward Waters College

Jacksonville, FL

www.ewc.edu

Everest University, Brandon

Tampa, FL

www.everest.edu

Johnson & Wales University, North
Miami

North Miami, FL

www.jwu.edu

Keiser University

Fort Lauderdale, FL (Main Campus)

www.keiseruniversity.edu

Lynn University

Boca Raton, FL

www.lynn.edu

Remington College, Tampa

Tampa, FL

www.remingtoncollege.edu/tampa

Southeastern University

Lakeland, FL

www.seuniversity.edu

## Georgia

Bauder College

Atlanta, GA

www.bauder.edu

Georgia College and State
University

Milledgeville, GA

www.gcsu.edu

## Hawaii

Hawaii Pacific University

Honolulu, HI

www.hpu.edu

University of Hawaii, West Oahu

Pearl City, HI

www.uhwo.edu

## Idaho

Boise State University

Boise, ID

www.boisestate.edu

## Illinois

Bradley University

Peoria, IL

www.bradley.edu

Concordia University

Chicago, IL

www.cuchicago.edu

Eureka College
Eureka, IL
www.eureka.edu

Greenville College
Greenville, IL
www.greenville.edu

Lewis University
Romeoville, IL
www.lewisu.edu

Millikin University
Decatur, IL
www.millikin.edu

Southern Illinois University,
  Carbondale
Carbondale, IL
www.siu.edu

Western Illinois University
Moline, IL
www.wiu.edu

Western Illinois University, Quad
  Cities
Moline, IL
www.wiu.edu/qc

Westwood College of Technology
Chicago, IL
www.westwood.edu

## Indiana

Indiana Business College

  Fort Wayne Campus
  Fort Wayne, IN
  www.ibcshools.edu

  Indianapolis Campus
  Indianapolis, IN
  www.ibcschools.edu

  Muncie Campus
  Muncie, IN
  www.ibcschools.edu

Indiana Institute of Technology
Fort Wayne, IN
www.indianatech.edu

Indiana University-Purdue
  University, Fort Wayne
Fort Wayne, IN
www.iupui.edu

Purdue University
West Lafayette, IN
www.purdue.edu

Purdue University, Calumet
Hammond, IN
www.calumet.purdue.edu

University of Indianapolis
Indianapolis IN
www.uindy.edu

## Iowa

Briar Cliff University
Sioux City, IA
www.briarcliff.edu

Kaplan University, Mason City
Mason City, IA
www.kucampus.edu

Mount Mercy College
Cedar Rapids, IA
www.mtmercy.edu

## Kansas

Central Christian College of Kansas
McPherson, KS
www.centralchristian.edu

MidAmerica Nazarene University
Olathe, KS
www.mnu.edu

Newman University
Wichita, KS
www.newmanu.edu

Washburn University
Topeka, KS
www.washburn.edu

## Kentucky

Beckfield College
Florence, KY
www.beckfield.edu

Bellarmine University
Louisville, KY
www.bellarmine.edu

Campbellsville University
Campbellsville, KY
www.campbellsville.edu

Thomas More College
Crestview Hills, KY
www.thomasmore.edu

Union College
Barbourville, KY
www.unionky.edu

University of Louisville
Louisville, KY
www.louisville.edu

## Louisiana

Louisiana College
Pineville, LA
www.lacollege.edu

Southwest University
Kenner, LA
www.southwest.edu

## Maine

Husson College
Bangor, ME
www.husson.edu

Thomas College
Waterville, ME
www.thomas.edu

University of Maine
Augusta, ME
www.uma.edu

**Maryland**
Frostburg State University
Frederick, MD
www.frostburg.edu

**Massachusetts**
American International College
Springfield, MA
www.aic.edu

Lasell College
Newton, MA
www.lasell.edu

Newbury College
Boston, MA
www.newbury.edu

Salem State College
Salem, MA
www.salemstate.edu

Springfield College
Springfield, MA
www.spfldcol.edu

Suffolk University
Boston, MA
www.suffolk.edu

University of Massachusetts
Amherst, MA
www.umass.edu

**Michigan**
Concordia University
Ann Arbor, MI
www.cuaa.edu

Grand Valley State University
Allendale, MI
www.gvsu.edu

Lake Superior State University
Sault Ste. Marie, MI
www.lssu.edu

Michigan State University
East Lansing, MI
www.msu.edu

University of Detroit Mercy
Detroit, MI
www.udmercy.edu

University of Michigan, Flint
Flint, MI
www.umflint.edu

## Minnesota

Concordia University, St. Paul
St. Paul, MN
www.csp.edu

Minnesota State University, Mankato
Mankato, MN
www.mnsu.edu

St. Mary's University of Minnesota
Minneapolis, MN
www.smumn.edu

Southwest Minnesota State
   University
Marshall, MN
www.southwest.msus.edu

Winona State University
Winona, MN
www.winona.edu

## Mississippi

Mississippi College
Clinton, MS
www.mc.edu

University of Mississippi
Lafayette, MS
www.olemiss.edu

## Missouri

Central Methodist University
Fayette, MO
www.centralmethodist.edu

Columbia College
Columbia, MO
www.ccis.edu

Culver-Stockton College
Canton, MO
www.culver.edu

Grantham University
Kansas City, MO
www.grantham.edu

Hannibal-LaGrange College
Hannibal, MO
www.hlg.edu

Harris-Stowe State University
St. Louis, MO
www.hssu.edu

Lincoln University
Jefferson City, MO
www.lincolnu.edu

Missouri Southern State University
Joplin, MO
www.mssu.edu

Missouri Valley College
Marshall, MO
www.moval.edu

Park University
Parkville, MO
www.park.edu

Saint Louis University
St. Louis, MO
www.slu.edu

Southwest Baptist University
Bolivar, MO
www.sbuniv.edu

University of Central Missouri
Warrensburg, MO
www.ucmo.edu

University of Missouri, Kansas City
Kansas City, MO
www.umkc.edu

## Montana
*None that offer BA degrees*

## Nebraska
Bellevue University
Bellevue, NE
www.bellevue.edu

Dana College
Blair, NE
www.dana.edu

Peru State College
Peru, NE
www.peru.edu

## Nevada
*None that offer BA degrees*

## New Hampshire
Granite State College
Concord, NH
www.granite.edu

Hesser College
Manchester, NH (and other
   campuses)
www.hesser.edu

## New Jersey
The College of New Jersey
Ewing, NJ
www.tcnj.edu

Georgian Court University
Lakewood, NJ
www.georgian.edu

Kean University
Union, NJ
www.kean.edu

Rutgers, The State University of
   New Jersey
New Brunswick, NJ
www.rutgers.edu

Thomas Edison State College
Trenton, NJ
www.tesc.edu

## New Mexico
Western New Mexico University
Silver City, NM
www.wnmu.edu

# Bachelor's Degrees in Criminal Justice and Law Enforcement

## New York

Adelphi University
Garden City, NY
www.adelphi.edu

City University of New York, John
    Jay College of Criminal Justice
New York, NY
www.jjay.cuny.edu

College of Saint Rose
Albany, NY
www.strose.edu

Iona College
New Rochelle, NY
www.iona.edu

Keuka College
Keuka Park, NY
www.keuka.edu

Long Island University, C.W. Post
    Campus
Brookville, NY
www.liu.edu

Marist College
Poughkeepsie, NY
www.marist.edu

Mercy College
New York, NY (and other campuses)
www.mercycollege.edu

Molloy College
Rockville Centre, NY
www.molloy.edu

Monroe College
Bronx, NY (and other campuses)
www.monroecollege.edu

New York Institute of Technology
New York, NY (and other campuses)
www.nyit.edu

Pace University
New York, NY
www.pace.edu

Roberts Wesleyan College
Rochester, NY
www.roberts.edu

Rochester Institute of Technology
Rochester, NY
www.rit.edu

Sage College of Albany
Troy and Albany, NY
www.sage.edu

St. John's University
Queens, NY
www.stjohns.edu

St. Thomas Aquinas College
Sparkill, NY
www.stac.edu

State University of New York, Canton
Canton, NY
www.canton.edu

## North Carolina

Brevard College
Brevard, NC
www.brevard.edu

Catawba College
Salisbury, NC
www.catawba.edu

Chowan University
Murfreesboro, NC
www.chowan.edu

Miller-Motte Technical College
Wilmington, NC
www.miller-motte.com

North Carolina Central University
Durham, NC
www.nccu.edu

Surry Community College
Dobson, NC
www.surry.edu

## North Dakota

University of Mary
Bismarck, ND
www.umary.edu

## Ohio

Ashland University
Ashland, OH
www.ashland.edu

Cedarville University
Cedarville, OH
www.cedarville.edu

Heidelberg College
Tiffin, OH
www.heidelberg.edu

Lake Erie College
Painesville, OH
www.lec.edu

Ohio Northern University
Ada, OH
www.onu.edu

Tiffin University
Tiffin, OH
www.tiffin.edu

Union Institute & University
Cincinnati, OH
www.tui.edu

University of Findlay
Findlay, OH
www.findlay.edu

Urbana University
Urbana, OH
www.urbana.edu

Youngstown State University

Youngstown, OH

www.ysu.edu

## Oklahoma

Mid-America Christian University

Oklahoma City, OK

www.macu.edu

Northeastern State University

Tahlequah, OK

www.nsuok.edu

Oklahoma City University

Oklahoma City, OK

www.okcu.edu

Rogers State University

Claremore, OK

www.rsu.edu

## Oregon

Portland State University

Portland, OR

www.pdx.edu

Southern Oregon University

Ashland, OR

www.sou.edu

Western Oregon University

Monmouth, OR

www.wou.edu

## Pennsylvania

Alvernia College

Reading, PA

www.alvernia.edu

Chestnut Hill College

Philadelphia, PA

www.chc.edu

Delaware Valley College

Doylestown, PA

www.delval.edu

Drexel University

Philadelphia, PA

www.drexel.edu

Gwynedd-Mercy College

Gwynedd Valley, PA

www.gmc.edu

Keystone College

La Plume, PA

www.keystone.edu

Lock Haven University of

Pennsylvania

Lock Haven, PA

www.lhup.edu

Mansfield University of Pennsylvania

Mansfield, PA

www.mansfield.edu

Marywood University
Scranton, PA
www.marywood.edu

Penn State
www.psu.edu
Abington Campus
Abington, PA
www.abington.psu.edu

Altoona Campus
Altoona, PA
www.aa.psu.edu

Beaver Campus
Monaca, PA
www.br.psu.edu

Berks Campus
Reading, PA
www.bk.psu.edu

Brandywine Campus
Media, PA
www.brandywine.psu.edu

DuBois Campus
DuBois, PA
www.ds.psu.edu

Erie, The Behrend College
    Campus
Erie, PA
www.erie.psu.edu

Fayette, The Eberly Campus
Uniontown, PA
www.fe.psu.edu

Greater Allegheny Campus
McKeesport, PA
www.ga.psu.edu

Hazleton Campus
Hazleton, PA
www.hn.psu.edu

Lehigh Valley Campus
Fogelsville, PA
www.lv.psu.edu

Mont Alto Campus
Mont Alto, PA
www.ma.psu.edu

New Kensington Campus
New Kensington, PA
www.nk.psu.edu

Schuylkill Campus
Schuylkill Haven, PA
www.sl.psu.edu

Shenango Campus
Sharon, PA
www.shenango.psu.edu

University Park (Main Campus)
University Park, PA
www.psu.edu

Wilkes-Barre Campus
Lehman, PA
www.wb.psu.edu

Worthington Scranton Campus
Dunmore, PA
www.sn.psu.edu

York Campus
York, PA
www.yk.psu.edu

Point Park University
Pittsburgh, PA
www.pointpark.edu

University of Pittsburgh
Bradford Campus
Bradford, PA
www.upb.pitt.edu

Greensburg Campus
Greensburg, PA
www.upg.pitt.edu

Villanova University
Villanova, PA
www.villanova.edu

Waynesburg University
Waynesburg, PA
www.waynesburg.edu

York College of Pennsylvania
York, PA
www.ycp.edu

**Puerto Rico**
Interamerican University of Puerto
Rico
www.inter.edu
Barranquitas Campus
Barranquitas, PR
www.br.inter.edu

Guayama Campus
Guayama, PR
www.guayama.inter.edu

Ponce Campus
Ponce, PR
www.ponce.inter.edu

Universidad Metropolitana
Cupey, PR
www.suagm.edu

Universidad del Este
Carolina, PR
www.suagm.edu

University of Puerto Rico, Carolina
Regional College
Carolina, PR
www.uprc.edu

**Rhode Island**
Johnson & Wales University,
Providence
Providence, RI
www.jwu.edu

Roger Williams University
Bristol, RI
www.rwu.edu

Salve Regina University
Newport, RI
www.salve.edu

## South Carolina

Anderson University
Anderson, SC
www.andersonuniversity.edu

The Citadel, The Military College of
   South Carolina
Charleston, SC
www.citadel.edu

Claflin University
Orangeburg, SC
www.claflin.edu

Limestone College
Gaffney, SC
www.limestone.edu

Morris College
Sumter, SC
www.morris.edu

South Carolina State University
Orangeburg, SC
www.scsu.edu

South University
Columbia, SC
www.southuniversity.edu

University of South Carolina
Columbia, SC
www.sc.edu

## South Dakota

*None that offer BA degrees*

## Tennessee

Austin Peay State University
Clarksville, TN
www.apsu.edu

East Tennessee State University
Johnson City, TN
www.etsu.edu

Lambuth University
Jackson, TN
www.lambuth.edu

Middle Tennessee State University
Murfreesboro, TN
www.mtsu.edu

University of Memphis
Memphis, TN
www.memphis.edu

University of Tennessee

Chattanooga Campus

Chattanooga, TN

www.utc.edu

Martin Campus

Martin, TN

www.utm.edu

## Texas

Abilene Christian University

Abilene, TX

www.acu.edu

Concordia University at Austin

Austin, TX

www.concordia.edu

Lubbock Christian University

Lubbock, TX

www.lcu.edu

Texas A&M University, Commerce

College Station, TX

www.tamu.edu

Texas College

Tyler, TX

www.texascollege.edu

Texas Southern University

Houston, TX

www.tsu.edu

University of Houston-Victoria

Victoria, TX

www.uhv.edu

University of Mary Hardin-Baylor

Belton, TX

www.umhb.edu

University of Texas

Brownsville Campus

Brownsville, TX

www.utb.edu

Pan American Campus

Edinburg, TX

www.utpa.edu

West Texas A&M University

Canyon, TX

www.wtamu.edu

Wiley College

Marshall, TX

www.wileyc.edu

## Utah

Utah Valley University (formerly Utah
Valley State College)

Orem, UT

www.uvu.edu

## Vermont

*None that offer BA degrees*

## Virginia

Averett University
Danville, VA
www.averett.edu

Bluefield College
Bluefield, VA
www.bluefield.edu

Hampton University
Hampton, VA
www.hampton.edu

Virginia Commonwealth University
Richmond, VA
www.vcu.edu

Virginia Intermont College
Bristol, VA
www.vic.edu

## Washington

*None that offer BA degrees*

## West Virginia

American Public University System
Charles Town, WV
www.apus.edu

Fairmont State University
Fairmont, WV
www.fairmontstate.edu

Mountain State University
   (formerly called The College of
   West Virginia)
Beckley, WV
www.mountainstate.edu

West Virginia Wesleyan College
Buckhannon, WV
www.wvwc.edu

## Wisconsin

Lakeland College
Sheboygan, WI
www.lakeland.edu

Marian College of Fond du Lac
Fond du Lac, WI
www.mariancollege.edu

University of Wisconsin, Platteville
Platteville, WI
www.uwplatt.edu

## Wyoming

*None that offer BA degrees*

# Appendix C

# Additional Sources of Information: Websites and Print Resources

## WEBSITES

dhs.gov
Official website of the Department of Homeland Security providing information on all that the DHS has to offer.

usa.gov
The United States government's official Web portal providing access to all the federal government's websites.

usajobs.gov
Official website source for federal government job announcements and Federal Resume Builder.

studentjobs.gov
Official website source for students interested in federal government job announcements and starting a career in government.

ourpublicservice.org
A nonprofit, non-partisan organization that works to revitalize federal government.

bls.gov
Official website of the Bureau of Labor and Statistics; is the government's fact-finding agency in the area of labor, economics, and statistics.

makingthedifference.org
Partnership for Public Service in cooperation with the federal government is the source for federal jobs and internships, where to find them, and how to get them.

ice.gov
Official website for U.S. Immigration and Customs Enforcement, the largest investigative agency in the Department of Homeland Security.

opm.gov
Official website for the Office of Personnel Management, the human resources arm of the federal government and managing agency of usajobs.gov and studentjobs.gov. It provides guidance on federal employment.

secretservice.gov
Official website for the United States Secret Service, one of the agencies in the Department of Homeland Security

911jobforums.com
A blog providing information about the federal government, employment, and application processes from people who have been there.

tsa.gov
Official website of the Transportation Security Administration in the Department of Homeland Security.

govcentral.com
Operated by monster.com; provides information about jobs with the federal government.

cbp.gov
Official website of U.S. Customs and Border Protection, one of the Department of Homeland Security's largest and most complex agencies.

military.com

Provides news and information for military personnel on jobs and transitioning to federal employment.

fletc.gov

Official website for the Federal Law Enforcement Training Center, the federal government's training center for Department of Homeland Security employees.

usfedgovjobs.com

Web blogging site, provides information about government employment.

workforamerica.com

Federal employment information website provides information on government agencies, advice, news, and government job search tools. Sponsored by careerbuilders.com.

whitehouse.gov

Official government website for the White House, providing information about issues affecting government including Homeland Security.

heritage.org

The Heritage Foundation, a public policy research institute providing information on the federal government, is committed to building an America where freedom, opportunity, prosperity, and civil society flourish.

careervoyages.gov

Official government website providing the opportunity to explore in-demand federal careers.

onecenter.org

Created for the U.S. Department of Labor, it is the nation's source for occupational information, containing data on hundreds of standardized and occupational specific descriptions, career assessments, and job tools.

resume-place.com

The Resume Place, Inc., and Kathryn Troutman, author of *Federal Resume Guidebook* published by JIST Works, provide an overall strategy for success in the federal hiring process.

federalgovernmentjobs.us
Is an alternative job announcement listing service utilized by some agencies. Some job announcements found here are not found on USAJOBS.GOV.

## PRINT RESOURCES

*Becoming a Border Patrol Agent*, LearningExpress, LLC, New York, 2009. This book details the day-to-day working conditions of the United States Border Patrol and contains a comprehensive look at the Border Patrol's entrance exam.

*Federal Resume Guide Book*, Fourth Edition, by Kathryn Kraemer Troutman. JIST Works, an imprint of JIST Publishing, Indianapolis, IN, 2007. Kathryn Troutman is a federal resume expert, career consultant, and government human resources career trainer. This is by far the most comprehensive book written on the federal application process detailing the writing of a federal resume and effective KSAs.

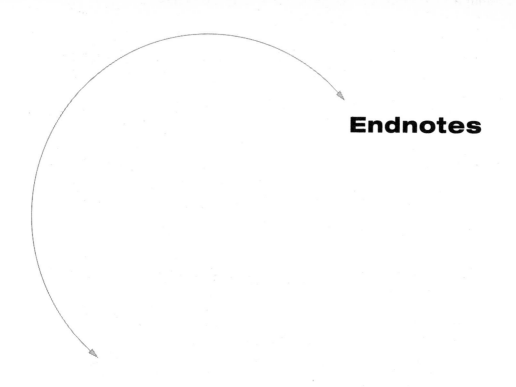

# Endnotes

## CHAPTER 1   WHY HOMELAND SECURITY?

1. Department of Homeland Security, Strategic Plan Fiscal Years 2008–2013, Sept. 16, 2008, http://www.dhs.gov/xlibrary/assets/DHS_StratPlan_FINAL_spread.pdf, Aug. 10, 2009.
2. Department of Homeland Security, Department Celebrates Five years, http://www.dhs.gov/xabout/history/gc_1206633633513.shtm, Aug. 10, 2009.
3. Department of Homeland Security, Strategic Plan, http://www.dhs.gov/xabout/strategicplan/, Aug. 10, 2009.
4. Department of Homeland Security, Department Subcomponents and Agencies, http://www.dhs.gov/xabout/structure/, Aug, 10, 2009.
5. Office of Personnel Management, Fact Book, http://www.opm.gov/feddata/factbook/2007/2007FACTBOOK.pdf, Aug. 18, 2009.
6. Office of Personnel Management, Fact Book, http://www.opm.gov/feddata/factbook/2007/2007FACTBOOK.pdf, Aug. 18, 2009.

7.  Office of Personnel Management, Fact Book, http://www.opm.gov/fed data/factbook/2007/2007FACTBOOK.pdf, Aug. 18, 2009.

8.  Partnership for Public Service, Where the Jobs Are/Mission Critical Opportunities for America, 2nd Edition, 2007.

9.  Office of Personnel Management, Fact Book, http://www.opm.gov/fed data/factbook/2007/2007FACTBOOK.pdf, Aug. 18, 2009.

## CHAPTER 2   MISSION SUPPORT CAREERS

1.  Department of Homeland Security, Directorate for Management, http://www.dhs.gov/xabout/structure/editorial_0096.shtm, Aug. 26, 2009.

## CHAPTER 3   LAW ENFORCEMENT CAREERS

1.  U.S. Customs and Border Protection, This is CBP, http://www.cbp.gov/xp/cgov/about/mission/cbp_is.xml, Sept. 03, 2009.

2.  U.S. Customs and Border Protection, CBP Mission Statement and Core Values, http://www.cbp.gov/xp/cgov/about/mission/guardians.xml, Sept. 03, 2009.

## CHAPTER 4   IMMIGRATION AND TRAVEL SECURITY CAREERS

1.  U.S. Citizenship and Immigration Services, USCIS Operating Performance, http://www.uscis.gov/files/nativedocuments/operating_performance_apr09.pdf, Sept. 10, 2009.

## CHAPTER 5   PREVENTION AND RESPONSE CAREERS

1.  U.S. Coast Guard, Coast Guard 2009 Snapshot 08/09, http://www.uscg.mil/top/about/doc/uscg_snapshot.pdf, Sept. 11, 2009.

2. Federal Emergency Management Agency, FEMA Strategic Plan Fiscal Years 2008-2013, Pg. 4, http://www.fema.gov/pdf/about/fy08_fema_sp_bookmarked.pdf, Sept. 15, 2009.

## CHAPTER 6 CUTTING EDGE CAREERS IN CYBER SECURITY

1. The Department of Homeland Security, US-CERT, United States Computer Emergency Readiness Team, IT Security Essential Body of Knowledge, A Competency and Functional Framework for IT Security Workforce Development, http://www.us-cert.gov/ITSecurityEBK/, Oct. 14, 2009.
2. The Department of Homeland Security, Secretary Napolitano Announces New Hiring Authority for Cyber Security Experts, October 01, 2009, http://www.dhs.gov/ynews/releases/pr_1254411508194.shtm, October 08, 2009.

## CHAPTER 8 CAREERS IN ACQUISITIONS

1. Department of Homeland Security, Office of Inspector General, Advisory Report: "Department of Homeland Security's Capabilities to Implement the American Recovery and Reinvestment Act of 2009," OIG-09-74, June 2009, http://www.dhs.gov/xoig/assets/mgmtrpts/OIG_09-74_Jun09.pdf, Sept. 20, 2009.
2. Acquisition Central, Federal Acquisition Regulation (FAR), Part 2, Subpart 2.101(b)(2), http://www.arnet.gov/far/current/html/Subpart%202_1.html, Sept. 18, 2009.
3. Partnership for Public Service, "Where the Jobs Are Mission Critical Opportunities for America," 2nd Edition-2007, PDF, Sec1:54, www.ourpublicservice.org, Sept 21, 2009.
4. Partnership for Public Service, Where the Jobs Are Mission Critical Opportunities for America, 2nd Edition-2007, PDF, Sec1:4, www.ourpublicservice.org, Sept 21, 2009.

## CHAPTER 9   WHAT ARE THE OPPORTUNITIES?

1.  Office of Personnel Management, "An Analysis of Federal Employee Retirement Data March 2008," http://www.opm.gov/feddata/Retirement PaperFinal_v4.pdf, Sept 23, 2009.
2.  Partnership for Public Service, "Where the Jobs Are 2009, Mission Critical Opportunities for America," http://wherethejobsare.org/WTJA/analysis/topfive.shtml, Sept. 30, 2009.
3.  The White House, Office of Budget and Management, President's Budget—Fact Sheets, United States Department of Homeland Security, http://www.whitehouse.gov/omb/fy2010_department_homeland/, Oct. 05, 2009.

## CHAPTER 10   FINDING YOUR CAREER FIT

1.  The Naval Postgraduate School Center for Defense and Homeland Security. http://www.chds.us/?about, Oct.16, 2009.
2.  "Colleges Offer Homeland Security Major." *USA Today*, Nov. 11, 2006.
3.  Department of Homeland Security. "DHS Announces $30 Million in Competitive Grants to Strengthen Preparedness Training." www.dhs.gov/xnews/releases/press_release_0779.shtm, Oct. 25, 2009.

## CHAPTER 11   FEDERAL RESUMES AND KSAs

1.  Office of Personnel Management, News Release September 10, 2008, "OPM Unveils End-To-End Hiring Roadmap, Initiative Designed to Streamline the Federal Hiring Process," http://www.opm.gov/news/opm-unveils-endtoend-hiring-roadmap,1430.aspx, Oct, 23, 2009.

## CHAPTER 12   OBTAINING A SECURITY CLEARANCE

1.  Willing, R., and J. Prados, "White House Looks for Faster Top-Secret Clearances." *USA Today*, Feb. 14, 2007.

2.  "Clearance Jobs, Security Clearance Frequently Asked Questions," http://www.clearancejobs.com/security_clearance_faq.pdf, Sept. 15, 2009.

3.  Defense Security Services, Frequently Asked Questions, https://www.dss.mil/GW/ShowBinary/DSS/psco/ps_faqs.html, Sept. 8 2009.

4.  Federal Bureau of Investigation, "Background Investigations, All FBI Employees Require Clearance," www.fbijobs.gov/52/asp, Sept. 20, 2009.

## CHAPTER 14   WHAT HAPPENS IF I CHANGE MY MIND?

1.  U.S. Bureau of Labor Statistics, "Career Planning the Second Time Around," www.opm.gov, Oct. 29, 2009.

2.  Partnership for Public Service, "Getting Onboard, a Model for Integrating and Engaging New Employees," May 2008, www.ourpublicservice.org, Oct. 29, 2009.

3.  Leigh Branham, *The 7 Hidden Reasons Employees Leave: How to Recognize the Subtle Signs and Act Before It's Too Late*, 2005, American Management Association, AMACOM Publishing.

# NOTES

# NOTES